# 108 Divya Desams: An Artist Journey

## Vol-1: 40 Chola Marvel

### Shanmugam palanI

notionpress
.com

INDIA · SINGAPORE · MALAYSIA

ISBN
Paperback  979-8-89498-364-6
Hardcase  979-8-89673-407-9

# Dedication

To **Velukkudi** Sri U. Ve. **Krishnan** Swamy

Who inspired me to explore and appreciate the sacred temples of the 108 Divya Desams. Your wisdom and dedication have been a beacon on my spiritual journey, leading me to a deeper understanding and connection with the divine.

To my beloved parents

Your sacrifices and resilience in the face of turbulent family situations have given us a better life and education. Moving away from the village to provide us with greater opportunities is a testament to your enduring love and dedication. Your efforts not only instilled in me the value of perseverance but also sparked the creative skills that have brought this book to life.

To my dear in-laws,

Your unwavering support and presence have been invaluable throughout this journey. Thank you for standing by us and providing the encouragement and strength we needed to make this book a reality.

With deepest gratitude and love,

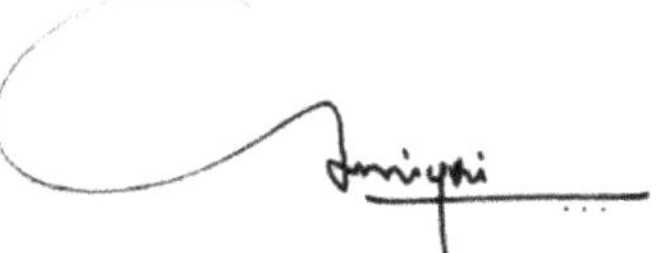

# Acknowledgments

To my beloved wife, Rajashree and Lovely Daughter Harshikashree

Your unwavering support and encouragement have been the foundation of this journey. It was your idea to transform my sketches into this book, and your belief in me that made it a reality. Thank you Raji and Harshu for standing by my side through every challenging moment and joyful discovery during our travels to all the temples.

Your love and companionship have been my strength and inspiration.

# Behind the Sketches

This book is a reflection of countless hours of dedication, research, and artistic passion. The journey of creating it was not just about visiting the sacred Divya Desams but also about immersing myself in their timeless history, intricate architecture, and spiritual essence.

Every sketch in this book carries a piece of my heart and soul, born from long hours of observation, attention to detail, and a desire to bring these divine abodes to life on paper. From navigating challenging terrains to enduring physically and emotionally testing moments, the path was often steep, yet deeply fulfilling.

The primary aim of this work is to serve as a beacon for spiritual seekers, heritage enthusiasts, and anyone who cherishes the magnificence of ancient art and architecture. I hope it inspires readers to embark on their own journey of discovering these divine spaces, not just through the pages of this book but in person as well.

It is important to note that certain Divya Desams consist of multiple temples or locations grouped together. In such cases, I have chosen to represent only one temple from the group to maintain simplicity and focus. This decision was not easy but was made to ensure the book's format remains consistent and accessible to the reader.

This endeavor has been one of the most challenging yet fulfilling experiences of my life. It is my humble offering to those who seek to understand and connect with the timeless legacy of the Divya Desams.

As I look back, I feel immense gratitude for the opportunity to create something that resonates with both my passion as an artist and my spiritual exploration. I hope this book inspires you as much as the process of creating it inspired me.

# CONTENTS

# 01 THIRUVARANGAM

- **Moolavar**: Sri Ranganatha Perumal or Periya Perumal

- **Utsavar**: Sri Namperumal, Sri Azhagiya Manavalan

- **Thaayar**: Sri Ranga Nayagi Thaayar

- **Vimanam**: Pranavakara Vimanam

- **Pushkarani**: Chandra Pushkarani

- **Prathyaksham**: Dharmavarma, Ravindharman, chandiran and Vibeeshanan

- **Location**: Thiruchirappalli, Srirangam

## Architectural Significance:

The Srirangam temple stands as the largest temple complex in India and ranks among the most extensive religious complexes globally. It is widely acknowledged as the largest operational Hindu temple in the world. This remarkable complex has been nominated for UNESCO World Heritage Site status and, in 2017, was honoured with the UNESCO Asia Pacific Award of Merit for cultural heritage conservation, marking a first for temples in Tamil Nadu.

Covering an area of 63 hectares (155 acres), the temple encompasses 54 shrines, 21 towers, 39 pavilions, and numerous water tanks. It is encircled by seven concentric enclosures known as prakarams or mathil suvar, with walls and gopurams that were built or reinforced post the 16th century. These fortifications stretch over six miles (32,592 feet or 9,934 meters). The temple is adorned with 17 major gopurams and a total of 21 towers. Notable features include the Ayiram Kaal Mandapam, a hall with 1,000 pillars, nine sacred water pools, and several smaller water bodies within the complex. This detailed and vast design highlights the temple's architectural splendour and its profound cultural significance.

## The Grandeur of Srirangam

Everything in Srirangam is grand:

- **Temple**: Periyakovil
- **Deity**: Periya Perumal
- **Goddess**: Periya Piratti
- **Hall**: Periya Thirumandapam
- **Festival**: Periya Thirunaal
- **Offering**: Periya Avasaram

## Srirangam Temple: The Heart of Divya Desams

Srirangam, also known as Periyakovil and Boolaga Vaikundam, holds a unique place among the 108 Divya Desams. It is the only Divya Desam where all 10 Azhwars sang Mangalasasanam, earning it the name "Padhinmar Padum Perumal." When someone mentions "Kovil" (temple), it is universally understood to refer to Srirangam.

## Kaveri Mahatmyam

Srirangam is situated between two branches of the Kaveri River: Vadathiru Kaveri (Kollidam) and Thenthiru Kaveri. The river encircles the temple like a garland, creating a natural island before merging downstream.

# The Arrival of Perumal in Srirangam

The legend of Srirangam's deity begins in Thiruparkadal (Milky Ocean) with a droplet forming the Pranavakara Vimanam. This Perumal was worshipped by Brahma in Sathyalogam. King Ikshvaku of Ayodhya, who could fly to Sathyalogam, saw the deity and requested Brahma to give him Perumal for Bhoologam (Earth). Brahma consented, and King Ikshvaku enshrined the deity on the banks of the Sarayu River, where successive kings worshipped him, including Lord Rama.

After his victory over Ravana, Lord Rama gifted the deity to Vibeeshanan (Ravana's brother) as a token of appreciation. On his journey to Sri Lanka, Vibhishana stopped at Srirangam for the grand Panguni Brahmotsavam. After the festival, he wished to continue his journey, but King Dharma Varma pleaded with him to leave the deity in Srirangam. Vibhishana, reluctant to part with the precious gift, consulted Perumal, who expressed his desire to stay in Srirangam. Perumal assured Vibhishana that he would face south towards Sri Lanka, blessing him from there. This divine arrangement remains to this day.

## Acharyas and Administration

Srirangam has been the residence of many revered acharyas, including Sri Nadhamunigal, Sri Alavandhar, and Sri Ramanujar. Sri Ramanujar established the temple's administration, rules, and regulations, shaping its current structure.

---

**Major Festivals:**

The annual 21-day festival conducted during the Tamil month of Margazhi (December–January) attracts 1 million visitors.

# 02 THIRUKKOZHI

Also called Nichulapuri or Nachiyar Kovil.

- **Moolavar:** Sri Azhagiya Manavaalan

- **Thaayar:** Sri Kamalavalli Naachiyaar. Also named "Urayoor Valli"

- **Pushkarani:** Sri Kamala Pushkarani

- **Vimanam:** Kalyana Vimanam

- **Mangalasasanam:** Kulasekara Azhwar - 1 Paasuram, Thirumangai Azhwar - 2 Paasuram

- **Prathyaksham:** Ravivarmaraja and all Devas

- **Location:** Situated in Urayoor, Trichy district in Tamil Nadu, 2 miles away from Trichy Junction.

## Etymology:

Once a fierce battle took place at this location between a fowl (known as "kozhi" in Tamil) and an elephant, culminating in the victory of the fowl with the blessing of Lord Rudra. Consequently, the area earned the name "Kozhiyur."

## Architectural Significance:

Dating back to the Sangam period, Nachiyar Kovil is one of the oldest temples in the region. It was established well before the 7th century and subsequently enhanced by the Chola, Pallava, and Nayak dynasties. During the Chola period, 'Urayoor' served as the capital city, and these rulers adorned the temple with intricate carvings, magnificent gopurams (gateway towers), and mythological sculptures. The temple, encircled by a granite wall, features a 239.5 feet tall rajagopuram, as illustrated in the depiction.

## Temple History:

The temple is also believed to be the place where King Ravivarmaraja worshipped the presiding deity.

It is believed that Lord Vishnu was pleased by the worship of Nandha Chola, who was childless. One day, he went hunting in the forest and found a girl child (incarnation of Lord Lakshmi) lying inside a 1,000-petal lotus. He adopted the girl and named her Kamalavalli, raising her as his own. Later, Lord Sriranga Perumal married her and lived there as Azhagiya Manavala Perumal.

## Special Highlights:

Nachiyar Kovil is the birthplace of the great Thirupaan Azhwar, who sang "Amalanadhipiran" as part of the Nalayira Divya Prabandham, which is considered the essence of the Vedas. It is also the birthplace of Pillai Uranga Valli Dasar, a disciple of Swami Ramanujar.

## Major Festivals:

On the 6th day of the Panguni Brahmotsavam, Lord Namberumal from Srirangam comes to Kozhiyur to offer blessings along with Kamal Valli Nachiyar, in a ceremony known as Serthi Seva.

# 03 THIRUKARAMBANUR

Also called as Uttamar Kovil and Pichandaar Kovil

- **Moolavar**: Sri Purushothaman

- **Thaayar**: Sri Pooranavalli Thaayar

- **Pushkarani**: Kadhamba Pushkarani

- **Vimanam**: Utthiyoga Vimanam

- **Mangalasasanam**: Thirumangai Azhwar - 1 Paasuram

- **Prathyaksham**: Kadhamba makarishi.

- **Location**: It is situated in Trichy, Tamil Nadu district, 8 km away from Trichy and 3.5 km from Srirangam, on Trichy to Salem highway.

## Architectural Significance:

The temple is believed to have been built by the Medieval Cholas of the late 8th century CE, with later contributions from Vijayanagara kings and Madurai Nayaks. A granite wall surrounds the temple, enclosing all its shrines, while the temple tank is located outside the main gateway.

## Temple History:

In ancient times, both Lord Brahma and Lord Shiva had five heads. Due to a disagreement, Lord Shiva plucked off one of Brahma's heads. However, Brahma's fifth head got stuck in Shiva's hand and refused to come off. The only way to remove the head was to feed it continuously until it was satisfied and willing to leave Shiva's hand.

Seeking relief, Lord Shiva arrived at Thirukarambanur to meet Poornavalli Thaayar, the consort of Lord Vishnu. Poornavalli Thaayar, known for her boundless compassion, offered food directly from her hand to Shiva. As she fed him, the fifth head of Brahma satiated and appeased, finally detached from Shiva's hand, freeing him from the burden.

To further test the devotion and virtues of Brahma, Lord Vishnu transformed himself into a Kadhamba tree (Kadhamba Maram) and created the sacred Kadhamba Theertham. This place became a site of immense spiritual significance, attracting divine presence and blessings.

# Special Highlights:

Thirumangai Azhwar stayed here and constructed the compound wall for Srirangam.

Lord Shiva, Lord Vishnu, and Lord Brahma, who are collectively called "Mum Murthy," are said to be found here in this temple.

Nagalinga Poo (flower), which is one of the famous and rare flowers, is found here and is used in poojas at this temple.

# Major Festivals:

During the auspicious month of Karthigai, a unique event occurs in Thirukarambanur. Both Lord Vishnu and Lord Shiva come together in a grand procession through the streets, symbolising the unity and harmony between the two deities. This event is celebrated with great fervour and devotion by the devotees.

# 04 THIRUVELLARAI

Also called **Shwetha giri**

- **Moolavar:** Sri Pundarikaksha Perumal

- **Thaayar:** Pangayarchelli Thaayar, Shenbaga Valli Thaayar

- **Pushkarani:** Varaaha Manikarnika Pushkarani

- **Vimanam:** Vimalaakkruthi Vimanam

- **Mangalasasanam:** PeriyAzhwar - 11 Paasurams, Thirumangai Azhwar - 13

- **Prathyaksham:** Sibi Chakaravarthi and Markandeya Maharishi.

- **Location:** The temple is located on the way between Trichy and Thuriyur main road.

## Architectural Significance

The temple, reportedly built by Sibi Chakravarthy, features two rock-cut caves with inscriptions dating from Nandivarman II and Dantivarman. It has two entrances, Utharayanya Vaasal and Dhakshinaya Vaasal, which are open alternately for six months each. A swastika-shaped temple tank, constructed around 800 CE, lies in the southwest corner with four gateways of 51 steps each. Believed to have been commissioned by Kamban Araiyan during Dantivarman's rule, it is now managed by the Tamil Nadu Archaeology Department.

## Temple History:

Once, Sibi Chakravarthi, a renowned king known for his righteousness and valor, visited Thiruvellarai with his troops. During their stay, one of his soldiers noticed a giant white boar running around the area. Intrigued by the unusual sight, the soldier attempted to catch the boar, but his efforts were in vain. He then informed the king about the elusive creature.

Sibi Chakravarthi, curious about the boar, began searching for it himself. The boar led him to a mysterious anthill (puttru). As Sibi approached the anthill, he saw Markandeya Rishi engrossed in deep meditation. The king inquired if the sage had seen the white boar. Markandeya Rishi responded, "Even I am waiting for something here, just like you. Why don't you perform abhishekam (ritual bathing) to the anthill?"

Following the sage's advice, Sibi Chakravarthi began performing abhishekam to the anthill.

As the water flowed over the anthill, the mud gradually washed away, revealing the divine form of Pundarikaksha Perumal. Markandeya Rishi praised Sibi Chakravarthi for his devotion and instructed him to establish a temple at that sacred spot. Additionally, he advised the king to bring 3700 Vaishnavites from his kingdom to Thiruvellarai.

Sibi Chakravarthi accepted the sage's advice and brought 3700 Vaishnavites to Thiruvellarai. However, upon arrival, he realized that one person was missing from the count. Worried, he began searching for the missing individual. At that moment, Perumal appeared before him and revealed, "I was included when you counted the Vaishnavites. You did not miss anyone." This divine revelation emphasized Perumal's wish to be counted as one among his devotees, highlighting his humility and love for his followers.

This story emphasises Perumal's humility and love for his devotees, showing how he desires to be included among them.

## Special Highlights:

Thirumanjanam for Bali Peedam.

## Major Festivals:

The Chariot Festival is the most prominent festival in the temple and surrounding villages. It is celebrated during the Tamil month of Panguni (March–April) when devotees pull the chariot around the streets of Thiruvellarai.

# 05 THIRU ANBIL

- **Moolavar:** Sri Sundaraja Perumal, also called Vadivazhagiya Nambi

- **Thaayar:** Sri Sundaravalli Thaayar

- **Pushkarani:** Mandooga Pushkarani - Kollidam

- **Vimanam:** Thaaraga Vimanam. Lots of sculptures are found here

- **Mangalasasanam:** Thirumazhisai Azhwar – 1

- **Prathyaksham:** Brahma, Shivan and Oorvasi

- **Location:** The temple is located in Trichy, Tamil Nadu on the North shore (Vadakarai) of the Kollidam River.

## Etymology:

Anbu - Love, il – house. The House of Love

## Temple History:

### The Story of Mandooka Muni

Once, in the celestial realms, Mandooka Muni was known for his intense penance. He performed his tapas (meditation) underwater to achieve higher spiritual wisdom. One day, while Mandooka Muni was deep in meditation, Dhurvasa Muni, a sage known for his temper, visited him. Absorbed in his penance, Mandooka Muni failed to acknowledge Dhurvasa Muni's presence and did not pay him the due respect.

Feeling insulted, Dhurvasa Muni cursed Mandooka Muni to become a frog. Seeking redemption from this curse, Mandooka Muni came to Thiruanbil, a sacred Divya Desam, to continue his penance and seek Lord Vishnu's grace.

Lord Vishnu, moved by Mandooka Muni's unwavering devotion, appeared before him as Vadivazhagiya Nambi. The lord blessed the sage and relieved him of his curse, restoring him to his original form. This divine act transformed Thiru Anbil into a place of immense spiritual significance.

## The Significance of Vadivazhagiya Nambi

Vadivazhagiya Nambi, the Utsava Moorthy (processional deity), is celebrated for his exquisite beauty and divine presence. The temple also venerates four forms of Lord Vishnu, collectively known as the Chaturvyuha (four emanations): Vasudeva, Sankarshana, Pradyumna, and Aniruddha, each representing different aspects of the divine strategy and cosmic functions.

## The Incident of Brahma's Head

In one of the earlier legends, it is said that Lord Shiva, in a fit of anger, chopped off one of Brahma's five heads. The severed head became stuck in Shiva's hand, and it was only through the grace of Lord Vishnu and his consort that the head was finally removed.

# Special Highlights:

Andal in Sitting posture.

## Major Festivals:

The Theerthavari festival celebrated in the Tamil month of Maasi (February–March) and Vaikuntha Ekadashi celebrated during the Tamil month of Margazhi (December–January) are the major festivals celebrated in the temple.

# 06 THIRUPPERNAGAR

Also called Koviladi, Appakudathan one of the Pancha Ranga Kshetram – Apala Rangam

- **Moolavar:** Sri Appakkudathan or Sri Appalaa Ranganathan

- **Thaayar:** Sri Kamala Valli

- **Pushkarani:** Indira Pushkarani

- **Vimanam:** Kanaka Vimana

- **Mangalasasanam:** PeriyAzhwar - 2 Paasurams, Thirumangai Azhwar 19 Paasurams, Thirumizhisai Azhwar – 1, Paasuram.NamaAzhwar - 11 Paasurams.

- **Prathyaksham:** Ubamannyu and Parasarar Bhattar.

- **Location:** This temple is on the way to Thiruvaiyaaru on Trichy to Kumbakonam highroad. People who are going to this temple should ask for "Koviladi".

## Architectural Significance:

The temple is considered to be of great antiquity, with various contributions from the Medieval Cholas over time. Constructed on an elevated platform, it is accessed via a flight of 21 steps. The rajagopuram (main gateway) features three tiers, and the temple complex includes a precinct surrounding the sanctum.

## Temple History:

King Upamanyu once angered Sage Durvasa, who was known for his unpredictable temper and cursed him. To lift the curse, the king was instructed to perform annadhanam, feeding 1,000 people daily. Following this directive diligently, the king organised annadhanam every day.

During one such ritual, Lord Perumal disguised himself as a hungry traveller and requested to be served first. Despite concerns about having enough food, the king respected the guest and served him. To the king's surprise, Perumal consumed all the prepared food and asked for appam, a favourite dish.

Despite worries about food shortage, King Upamanyu prepared and served appam. Perumal then revealed his divine form as Appakudathan Perumal and praised the king's devotion. Touched by the king's selflessness, Perumal not only lifted the curse but also blessed the kingdom with prosperity.

In gratitude, a temple was built in honour of Appakudathan Perumal, commemorating this miraculous event and divine intervention.

## The Legend of Kamalavalli Thaayar and the Parijatha Flower

Kamalavalli Thaayar, consort of Appakudathan Perumal, desired the celestial Parijatha flower known for its divine beauty and fragrance. She asked Perumal to bring it from heaven to Earth. Perumal requested Indra, the king of Devas, who refused, deeming the flower too divine for humans and sending a thunderbolt in anger.

While reclining, Perumal effortlessly caught the thunderbolt with his left hand, neutralising its power. This showcased his supreme strength and protection over his devotees. The story highlights Perumal's deep love for Kamalavalli Thaayar, fulfilling her wishes despite opposition from Indra. It underscores divine grace and Perumal's commitment to his consort's happiness and well-being.

## Major Festivals:

The chariot festival is the most prominent festival in the temple and surrounding villages. It is celebrated during the Tamil month of Panguni (April–May); devotees pull the temple chariot housing the festival deity around the streets of Koviladi.

# 07 THIRUKKANDIYUR

Also called Panja Kamala Kshetram

- **Moolavar:** Sri Hara Sabha Vimochana Perumal and Bali Natha Perumal

- **Utsavar:** Sri Kamalanathan

- **Thaayar:** Sri Kamala valli Thaayar.

- **Pushkarani:** Kabaala Moksha Pushkarani.

- **Vimanam:** Kamalakkruthi Vimanam

- **Mangalasasanam:** Thirumangai Azhwar - 1 Paasuram.

- **Prathyaksham:** Agathiya Munivar.

- **Location:** The temple is situated 6 miles away from Tanjore, 2 miles from Thiruvayyaaru.

## Temple History:

Lord Shiva, one of the "Mummoorthy" deities, was cursed when he pinched Lord Brahma's head, causing it to stick to his hand. This resulted in the "Brahmahathi Thosham" curse, making Shiva lose all his wealth and live a life of begging, earning him the name "Pikshandavar." Eventually, he was freed from the curse.

At this temple, Lord Vishnu, in the reclining posture facing East, represents the place where Shiva received redemption. The temple is called "Thirumurthy Kshetram" because it showcases all three deities—Shiva, Brahma, and Vishnu—indicating their interconnected roles in this legend.

The moral of this story is that even gods must face consequences for their actions, as demonstrated by Shiva's penance. This principle is deeply embedded in the temple's history and teachings.

The temple features separate shrines for Sriman Narayanan and Brahma Devan. Opposite is the Brahma Sirakandeeswarar Koil, named for the severed head incident. The site is also known as Kandiyoor.

Mahabali worshipped this Perumal.

## Major Festivals:

Four major festivals are celebrated in the temple, namely, the Panguni Brahmmotsavam, celebrated during the Tamil month of Panguni (March–April), Aipasi Pavithra Utsavam in Aipasi (October–November), Vaikunta Ekadashi in Margazhi (December–January), and Karthikai Deepam in Karthikai (November–December).

# 08 THIRUKKOODALOOR

Also called as Varaha Kshetram

- **Moolavar:** Sri Jagath Rakshaka Perumal, Vayam Katha Perumal, Aaduthurai Perumal

- **Thaayar:** Padmasini (Pushpavalli) Thaayar.

- **Pushkarani:** Chakkara Theertham - Cauvery Nadhi.

- **Vimanam:** Suttha sathva Vimanam.

- **Mangalasasanam:** Thirumangai Azhwar - 10 Paasurams.

- **Prathyaksham:** Nanthaga Maharishi.

- **Location**: It is situated in Tanjore district in Tamil Nadu, 6 Kms away from Ayyampettai, 7 miles away from Thiruvayyaaru - Kumbakkonam.

## Etymology:

After reaching this sthalam, the River Cauvery regained its special significance and holiness.

Koodal + oor = Koodaloor. "Koodal" means joining or merging together at the same place. Since the Cauvery converges in this Kshetram, it is also called "Sangama Kshetram," where "Sangamam" signifies coming together. The one who saved Boomadevi (Vayyam). Hence, the name Vayyankatha Perumal.

## Temple History:

### Story of Ambarisha Maharaja and Durvasa Muni

Ambarisha Maharaja, a descendant of Lord Sri Rama, was renowned for his devotion to Lord Vishnu and strict observance of the Ekadashi Vratham, fasting from Ekadashi until Dwadasi. On one Dwadasi, Durvasa Muni visited the king, who invited him for a meal after his bath. Durvasa Muni took a long time, leaving the king in a dilemma as he had to break his fast within a specified time but couldn't eat before his guest. Ambarisha drank water to symbolically end his fast, upholding his dharma to both Vishnu and the sage.

When Durvasa Muni returned and discovered this, he was enraged and cursed the king. Vishnu's divine discus, Sudarshana Chakra, protected Ambarisha and chased Durvasa Muni. The sage sought refuge from Brahma, Shiva, and Vishnu, but they advised him to seek forgiveness from Ambarisha. Realising his mistake, Durvasa begged for forgiveness, and the compassionate king prayed to Vishnu, who withdrew the Sudarshana Chakra.

### Ambarisha Maharaja's Devotion and the Temple Construction

Ambarisha Maharaja, a descendant of Lord Sri Rama, built a grand temple in Thirukoodalur to honour Jagathrakshakan Perumal, showcasing his devotion to Lord Vishnu. Over time, a severe flood buried the temple under sand and debris, and it was lost. Centuries later, Queen Mangammal, known for her piety, had a vivid dream in which Lord Vishnu revealed the temple's location and commanded her to restore it. Following the divine vision, she excavated and renovated the temple, reviving its former splendour. Devotees could once again worship Jagathrakshakan Perumal. In recognition of her devotion and role in the temple's restoration, a shrine dedicated to Rani Mangammal was built within the temple complex, symbolising her piety and divine guidance.

## Special Highlights

Koothadum Anjaneya, Narthana Anjaneyar

பரமபதவாசல்

# 09 THIRUKAVITHALAM

Also known as Kapisthalam, one among the 5 Krishna Kshetram

- **Moolavar:** Sri Gajendra Varadhan

- **Thaayar:** Sri Ramamani Valli (Potramaraiyaal).

- **Pushkarani:** Gajendra Pushkarani, Kabila Theertham.

- **Vimanam:** Gadhanakkruthi Vimanam.

- **Mangalasasanam:** Thirumangai Azhwar - 1 Paasuram

- **Prathyaksham:** Anjaneya and Bhaktha Elephant Gajendra.

- **Location:** It is situated in Tanjore district, Tamil Nadu, two miles away from Tanjore-Papanasam Railway Station. Kapisthalam Temple is situated between the sacred rivers Kaveri and Kollidam.

## Etymology:

Kavithalam - "Kavi" means poet - All the poets sang together; hence, the name ThiruKavithalam. It is also called Kapisthalam - "Kapi" meaning Monkey - Perumal gave Prathyaksham: Lord Anjaneya, and hence the temple is also called Kapistalam.

## Architectural Significance:

The temple is believed to have been built by the Medieval Cholas of the late 9th century CE, with later contributions from Vijayanagar kings and Madurai Nayaks. A granite wall surrounds the temple, enclosing all its shrines and bodies of water.

## Temple History:

### The Legend of Anjaneya's Tapas:

Anjaneya (Hanuman) performed intense penance here out of deep devotion to Lord Vishnu. He ardently desired to witness the divine event of Gajendra Moksha in this sacred temple.

### The Story of Gajendra Moksha:

King Indradyuman, known for his devotion, was once cursed to be reborn as an elephant named Gajendra due to neglecting sages Agastya and Durvasa. One day, while drinking from a pond, Gajendra was trapped by a crocodile. Despite his strength, he struggled for 1,000 years until he surrendered and prayed to Lord Vishnu for help. Touched by Gajendra's prayers, Vishnu appeared on Garuda and saved him by killing the crocodile with his discus.

Deep in penance at Kapisthalam, Anjaneya yearned to witness Gajendra Moksham. Moved by his devotion, Vishnu appeared as Gajendra Varadhan on Garuda, fulfilling Anjaneya's wish to witness the divine event. .

## Special Highlights:

Kapisthalam Temple, situated between the sacred rivers Kaveri and Kollidam, commemorates this divine interaction. The temple stands as a symbol of devotion, showcasing the Lord's readiness to bless his devotees and fulfil their sincere desires.

## Major Festivals:

The Gajendra Moksha Leela, celebrated in the Tamil month of Adi (July–August), Chariot Festival during the Tamil month of Vaikasi (May–June) on Visakam star, and Brahmotsavam are the major festivals celebrated in the temple.

# 10 THIRUPULLABHOOTHANGUDI

- **Moolavar:** Sri Valvil Raman

- **Thaayar: Sri** Potramaraiyaal (Sri Hemambujavalli).

- **Pushkarani:** Grithara Pushkarani, Jatayu Pushkarni

- **Vimanam:** Sobhana Vimanam.

- **Mangalasasanam:** Thirumangai Azhwar - 10 Paasurams.

- **Prathyaksham:** For himself Chakravarthy Thirumangan Ramar and King Kiruthra

- **Location:** This Divyadesam is situated in Tanjore district, Tamil Nadu, 3 miles away from Swami Malai.

## Architectural Significance:

Constructed in the South Indian style of architecture, the temple was built by the Medieval Cholas with additions from later kings. The temple is in Pullaboothangudi, a small village, 8 km away from Kumbakonam and 3 km from Swamimalai.

## Etymology:

The temple is called "Pullam Kudi" because "pull" refers to the bird family, and "kudi" means residence. Pushkarani here is named "Kiruthra Pushkarani" after purifying Kiruthrajan, who performed penance here and had a vision of Valvil Raman in Bujangha Sayanam.

Thirupullamboothangudi is revered as the place where Lord Rama performed the final rites for the great eagle, Jatayu. Jatayu, a devout follower and ally of Lord Rama, had sacrificed his life trying to rescue Sita from Ravana. In recognition of his loyalty and bravery, Lord Rama honoured Jatayu by performing the last rites at this sacred site.

After completing the ritual, Lord Rama, weary from his journey and the emotional farewell to Jatayu, decided to rest. He lay down with his bow by his side, embodying both his warrior spirit and his compassionate heart.

Thirumangai Azhwar, one of the twelve revered Azhwars known for their devotion and poetic hymns in praise of Lord Vishnu, arrived at Thirupullamboothangudi. As he approached, he saw a man resting with a bow and mistook him for an ordinary person.

Unperturbed, Lord Rama, in his infinite grace, realised that Thirumangai Azhwar had not recognised him. The Lord thought, "How can Thirumangai Azhwar pass by without singing praises of me?" To reveal his divine identity, Lord Rama appeared before Thirumangai Azhwar in his majestic form with four hands, holding the conch (shankha) and discus (chakra), along with the bow.

Awestruck and filled with devotion, Thirumangai Azhwar realised his mistake and immediately composed and sang hymns in praise of Lord Rama. This divine encounter deepened the bond between the devotee and the Lord, further immortalising the sacredness of Thirupullamboothangudi.

## Special Highlights:

The temple is the only place where Rama is depicted with four hands, with two of the hands holding the conch and discus.

## Major Festivals:

There are weekly, monthly, and fortnightly rituals performed in the temple. Vaikuntha Ekadashi, celebrated during the Tamil month of Margazhi (December–January), is the major festival celebrated in the temple.

# 11 THIRU AADANOOR

- **Moolavar:** Sri Ranganatha Perumal, Sri Aandu Alakkum Ayan

- **Thaayar:** Sri Ranganayaki Thaayar

- **Pushkarani:** Surya Thertham

- **Vimanam:** Pranavakara Vimanam

- **Mangalasasanam:** Kulasekhara Azhwar - 1 Paasuram

- **Prathyaksham:** Thirumangai Azhwar and Kamadhenu

- **Location:** The temple is located in Olaipadi, a small village in Kumbakonam, Tamil Nadu. 2 miles away from Swami Malai Railway station and in between Kumbakonam

## Temple History:

Once, Mahalakshmi's garland came to a woman's hand. She offered the garland to saint Dhuruvasa; Dhuruvasa thought about that was he would do with this Garland as a saint. Hence, he gave it to Lord Indra.

Lord Indra took the garland and put it to an elephant. The elephant didn't know about the importance of the garland and stamped it on its feet. So Indra got cursed.

He lost all this wealth and came to Sridevi Nachiyar. She said I would be born as Bhargavi for Bhrihu Maharshi and would get married to Lord Vishnu. You come to our thirukalyanam, and when you see our marriage, you will get all the wealth back.

Thirumangai Azhwar was the one who built the compound wall - After constructing the great wall he has to give wages to the workers. He did not have any money and was confused.

Perumal said, don't worry; I will give you the compensation to come to Aadanoor.

When he came to Thiruaadanoor, a trader came in front of Azhwar. Perumal sent me the required money and started giving sand to Azhwar.

Those who worked hard will see this as gold; the ones who didn't will see only sand. Everyone started to see only sand and started to complain to Azhwar that he was trying to cheat people. Azhawar went back to the trader and started asking if you were trying to cheat me. He started to chase him. While running, the trader noted down the amount of sand he had given Azhawar. He ran inside the temple and lay down along with the measure and the notebook. Lord Agni did tapas to get out of the curse.

This temple is being administered by Ahobilam mutt.

## Special Highlights:

One can see a measuring cup along with the Perumal in the Garbagraha.
On his left hand, with a Olai Chuvadi and a writing pen.

## Major Festivals:

The major festival of the temple, the Brahmotsavam, is celebrated during the Tamil month of Vaikasi (May - June). The major festival of the temple, the Brahmotsavam, is celebrated during the Tamil month of Vaikasi (May - June).

# 12 THIRU KUDANDAI

Kumbakonam Bhaskara Kshetram This Divya Desam in Kumbakonam includes three important temples: Sarangapani, Chakrapani, and Ramaswamy.

- **Moolavar:** Sri Sarangapani. Aara Amudhan.

- **Thaayar:** Sri Komalavalli Thaayar.

- **Pushkarani:** Hema Pushkarani (Potramarai Kulam). Cauvery Nadhi, Arasalaaru.

- **Vimanam:** Vaidega Vimanam

- **Moolavar:** Sri Chakrapani Perumal Depicted with the Sudarshana Chakra, signifying protection and divine energy.

- **Thaayar:** Sri Vijayavalli Thaayar

- **Pushkarani:** Chakra Theertham

- **Vimanam:** Vijayakoti Vimana

- **Moolavar:** Sri Ramaswamy Sita, Lakshmana, and Hanuman, highlighting the Ramayana epic

- **Thaayar:** Sri Seetha Devi

- **Pushkarani:** Sarayu Pushkarani

- **Vimanam:** Pushpaka

- **Mangalasasanam:** Sri Aandal - 1 Paasuram, PeriyAzhwar - 3 Paasurams, Thirumizhisai Azhwar - 7 Paasurams, BoothatAzhwar - 2 Paasurams, PeiyAzhwar - 2 Paasurams, NammAzhwar - 11 Paasurams, Thirumangai - 25 Paasurams.

- **Prathyaksham:** Hema Maharishi

- **Location**: This temple lies in the Kumbakonam. It's about 1 1/2 miles away from Kumbakkonam railway station.

# Architectural Significance:

Sarangapani Temple is the largest Vishnu temple in Kumbakonam, boasting the tallest temple tower in the town at 173 feet (53 meters). Enclosed by a massive wall, the temple complex includes all its water bodies except for the Potramarai tank. The main gateway, or rajagopuram, features eleven tiers adorned with religious figures and stories.

The temple is designed in the form of a chariot drawn by horses and elephants, symbolizing Sarangapani's descent from heaven. The central shrine, accessible through a 100-pillared hall, has a chariot-shaped sanctum guarded by Dwarapalakas. Inside the sanctum, the image of Sarangapani is depicted in a reclining posture, accompanied by images of Hemarishi, Lakshmi, and festival deities. There are two stepped entrances, Utharayana Vaasal and Dhakshanayana Vaasal, which open seasonally.

# Temple History:
## Creation of Kumbakonam

Lord Brahma collected all the seeds of evolution in a pot and saved them until the time of creation, keeping the pot safely in the Himalayas. The pot travelled from the Ganga River through many rivers and finally reached the Cauvery River. As it rolled upside down, the seeds spilled out. Lord Vishnu seized this opportunity to start creating life on Earth.

## Brihu Muni and Maha Lakshmi

Brihu Muni, in a fit of anger, kicked Lord Vishnu in the chest, where Goddess Maha Lakshmi resides. Upset, Maha Lakshmi left and went to Kolhapur to perform tapas (penance). Lord Vishnu also did tapas under an ant-hill to reunite with her.

## Promise to Akasharaja

Meanwhile, Lord Vishnu had promised Akasharaja that he would marry his daughter. Maha Lakshmi, still in Kolhapur, became angry upon hearing this and chased

Lord Vishnu. He fled and hid in a bunker in Kumbakonam, where he is now worshipped as Badhala Srinivasa Perumal in the Saranga Pani temple.

## Subduing Surya's Pride

To humble Surya (the Sun), Lord Vishnu sent his Sudarshana Chakra, which created the Chakra Theertham. This theertham reduces the heat caused by the sun. Therefore, Lord Vishnu appears here as Chakrapani, along with Vijayavalli Nayaki and Sudarsana Valli.

## Lord Rama and the Bow

During the Pattabishekam (coronation ceremony), Lord Rama gave his bow to his brother Lakshmana. Therefore, in the Ramanathaswamy Temple, Rama is depicted without his bow, while Lakshmana carries two bows.

# Special Highlights:

Naadamunigal and Divya Prabandham: In the 9th century, Naadamunigal compiled the scattered Divya Prabandham. After hearing a paasuram starting with "Aara Amudhey," he prayed at Saarangapani Temple, found the complete set of 4000 verses, and organised them. Hence, this temple is considered the birthplace of Nalayira Divya Prabandham.

## Major Festivals:

There are various festivals in this temple throughout the year, and some of the major ones are Akshaya Tritiyai - 12 Garuda Sevai, Chaitra Brahma Utsavam: April – May, Sri Jayanthi - Uriyadi Utsavam: August – September, Navaratri Utsavam - Saraswathi Puja - Pakal Pattu - Ira Pattu.

# 13 THIRUVINNAGAR

Also known as Uppiliappan Koyil

- **Moolavar:** Sri Oppiliappan, Sri Lavanavarjitha Swamy

- **Thaayar:** Sri Bhoomidevi Naachiyaar

- **Pushkarani:** Ahorathra pushkarani. Aarthi pushkarani.

- **Vimanam:** Vishnu Vimanam - Sudha Anandha Vimanam.

- **Mangalasasanam:** PeyAzhwar - 2 Paasurams, NammAzhwar - 11 Paasurams, Thirumangai Azhwar - 34 Paasurams.

- **Prathyaksham:** Markandeya Maharishi

- **Location:** This temple lies at Thirunageswaram in Tanjore district, Tamil Nadu. It is about 4 miles away from Kumbakonam and a mile away from Thirunageswaram railway station.

## Etymology:

Also known as Uppiliappa Koyil, this temple is also known as Agasa Kshetram, meaning "Vaikunda Nagaram" or the city of Vaikunta. It holds a special significance for devotees who cannot visit Thirumala, as visiting ThiruVinagar is believed to be equally auspicious. Perumal here is known as Opilla Appan, which means "nothing can be equated to Him," emphasising His unparalleled greatness.

## Architectural Significance:

The temple is believed to be of significant antiquity, initially established by the Medieval Cholas in the late 8th century CE, with later contributions from the Thanjavur Nayaks. The temple features a five-tiered rajagopuram (gateway tower), a granite wall, and contains two inscriptions from the Chola period indicating generous gifts of a gold jewel inlaid with gems and pearls to the temple from the Chola king Parakesarivarman, also known as Rajendra Chola I (1012–44 CE).

Another inscription records a gift of land to the temple in the 14th year of the reign of Chola king Rajaraja Rajakkesarivarman I.

Significant additions were made to the temple by Govinda Dikshitar, the minister of successive Nayak rulers, Achuthappa Nayak (1560–1614) and Raghunatha Nayak (1600–34)

## The Story of Markandeyar and Nachiyar

Mrikandu Maharishi's son, Markandeyar, had a daughter named Nachiyar. On a significant day in the month of Panguni, on the auspicious day of Ekadesi Thiruvonam, Perumal appeared as an elderly man and asked Mrikandu Maharishi for his daughter's hand in marriage. The Maharishi expressed concern, saying his daughter was so young she didn't even know salt was needed in cooking.

In response, Perumal decided that no salt (lavana) would be added to the food in this place, symbolising the unique attribute of the temple.

## Marriage of Nachiyar

The marriage talks for Nachiyar began in the month of Panguni, on the day of Thiruvonam, and continued until Aipasi Thiruvonam, lasting almost 11 months before the marriage was solemnised.

> **Major Festivals:**
>
> One of the important events at this temple is the Sravana Deepam, a significant festival that draws many devotees.

# 14 THIRUNARAYUR

Also called Nachiyar Kovil

- **Moolavar:** Thirunarayur Nambi.

- **Thaayar:** Sri Vanjulavalli Naachiyar

- **Pushkarani:** Mani mukthi Nadhi Theertham, Aniruddha Theertham, Pradhyumna Theertham, Samba Theertham, Sankarshana Theertham.

- **Vimanam:** Srinivasa Vimanam.

- **Mangalasasanam:** Thirumangai Azhwar-110 Paasurams.

- **Prathyaksham:** Medavi Munivar and Brahma devan.

- **Location:** This temple lies in the Tanjore district of Tamil Nadu. It is about 6 miles from Kumbakonam.

## Architectural Significance:

The temple is believed to have been built by King Kochengat Cholan, who is renowned for constructing 70 temples dedicated to Shiva, with Thirunaraiyur being the only Vishnu temple he built. The temple features a five-tiered rajagopuram on the eastern side, rising to a height of 75 feet (23 meters).

## Temple History:

### Thirumangai Azhwar's Transformation:

Thirumangai Azhwar, originally Neelan, transformed into a revered Azhwar due to his love for Kumudavalli, who set two marriage conditions:

1. He must undergo Pancha Samskaram, the five-fold purification rite.
2. He must offer Annadhanam (free meals) to 1,000 people daily for a year.

Determined, Neelan sought Pancha Samskaram, but as a military leader, people were afraid to perform it. Seeking divine help at Thirunarayur Temple, Lord Vishnu performed the rite himself, marking Neelan's initiation with divine symbols. This transformed him into Thirumangai Azhwar, fulfilling Kumudavalli's first condition and starting his path of devotion and service.

## The Stone Garuda and His Miraculous Weight:

In Thirunarayur Temple, the stone idol of Garuda, Lord Vishnu's vehicle, has a unique legend. Garuda performed penance here, and Lord Vishnu granted him the boon to eternally reside in the temple. As a result, Garuda took a stone form to stay in the sacred premises. To honour Garuda, the temple conducts a special ritual called "Anudha Kalam" and two annual Garuda Utsavams (festivals). During these festivals, Garuda is taken out in procession. Initially, eight devotees carry the Garuda Vahana, but as they proceed, the number of carriers doubles from 8 to 64, with Garuda's weight miraculously increasing at each mandapam (hall). On the return journey, the number of carriers decreases, showcasing divine intervention. This miraculous event attracts many devotees, highlighting Garuda's divine presence and blessings.

## Major Festivals:

Garuda Sevai is celebrated during the Tamil month of Panguni (March–April). During both these festivals, the festive images of Kal Garuda are taken around the streets of the temple. Vasanthotsavam, or spring festival, is celebrated during the Tamil month of Vaikasi (May–June). The Thirukalyana Utsavam, or the wedding festival, is celebrated in the 100-pillared hall during the Tamil month of Aavani (September–October). As per hagiographical records, it is believed that the Vaikhasana form of worship was originally practiced, and the temple started following the Panchratra form of worship after the advent of Saint Ramanuja.

# 15 THIRUCHERAI

## Also called as Pancha Sara Kshetram

- **Moolavar:** Sri Saranathan Perumal.

- **Thaayar:** Sri Saranayaki (Sara Naachiyaar).

- **Pushkarani:** Sara Pushkarani.

- **Vimanam:** Sara Vimanam.

- **Mangalasasanam:** Thirumangai Azhwar - 13 Paasurams.

- **Prathyaksham:** Kaveri Thaayar and Markendeya Maharishi.

- **Location:** This temple lies in the Tanjore district of Tamil Nadu. It is 7 miles from Kumbakonam and 3 miles from Naachiyar Kovil.

## Architectural Significance:

This temple, estimated to be 500 to 1,000 years old, features inscriptions from Chola Parakesari Varman (906-946 AD) and Babasahib of Madavipallam (1728–38), detailing various grants. Contributions from the Medieval Cholas, Vijayanagara Empire, and Madurai Nayaks highlight its significant antiquity.

After the Vijayanagar Empire's fall, Alagiya Manavala Naicker planned a Rajagopala Swamy temple in Mannarkudi, appointing Narasa Boopalan to gather black stones. A devout Saranatha Perumal worshipper, Boopalan, secretly constructed a temple in Thirucherai using stones meant for Mannarkudi. When discovered, he quickly built the temple overnight, adding a

Rajagopala Swamy shrine. The king, pleased, funded the temple's completion.

## Etymology:

Thirucherai is also called Pancha Sara Kshetram. Sara Kshetram, Saranatha Perumal, Sara Nayagai thayar, Sara Vimanam, Sara Pushkarani. Saram means sample.

## Temple History:

### The Boon of River Kaveri

At the foothills of the Vindhya Mountains, seven river goddesses were performing penance. The forest king saluted them all simultaneously, sparking a dispute between Ganga and Kaveri over who was honoured. Ganga claimed the salute, and the king reluctantly agreed, angering Kaveri. To prove her worth, Kaveri undertook rigorous penance.

Lord Vishnu, moved by her devotion, appeared as a child. Unsatisfied, Kaveri asked for more proof. Vishnu revealed his cosmic form, Vishvaroopam, but Kaveri sought further affirmation. Finally, Vishnu appeared as Vaikunta Pathi, the Lord of Vaikuntha, satisfying Kaveri. He then granted her a boon: Kaveri wished to be considered equal to Ganga. Vishnu assured her that when he manifests as Ranganatha Swamy in Srirangam, she would gain the same reverence as Ganga by flowing past and touching his feet, establishing her divine status alongside Ganga.

# Special Highlights:

Peruma is with 5 Thaayars inside the garbhagraham: Sri Devi, Bho Devi, Neela Devi, Maha Lakshmi, Sara Nayaki. Vanavasa Ramar can be seen in the temple with a beautiful statue.

# Major Festivals:

Serthi Utsava with all the 5 Thaayars

The major festival, the twelve-day Brahmotsavam, is celebrated during the Tamil month of Thai (January–February). It is believed that only on the auspicious day of the Pushya star of the month did Vishnu descend from Vaikuntam to Earth to bestow Kaveri. Rathotsavam, the temple car, is drawn during the ninth day of the festival.

# 16 THIRUKKANNAMANGAI

Thirukkannamangai Temple (Bhaktavatsala Perumal Temple). This temple is one of the Panchakanna (Krishnaranya) Kshetrams. Kannan refers to Krishna, the avatar of Vishnu, while pancha means five and Kshetrams refers to holy places.

- **Moolavar:** Sri Bhaktavatsala Perumal Temple, Perum Pura Kadal, Brihat Bahi sindu, Patharavi Perumal

- **Thaayar: Sri** Abisheka Valli Thaayar

- **Pushkarani:** Darisana Pushkarani

- **Vimanam:** Utpala Vimanam

- **Mangalasasanam:** Thirumangai Azhwar - 14 Paasurams.

- **Prathyaksham:** Lord Varuna and Romasa Munivar.

- **Location:** 5-6 miles from Thiruvarur

## Architectural Significance:

The temple believed to date back to the late 9th century CE, was initiated by the Medieval Cholas and later enhanced by the Thanjavur Nayaks. It features three inscriptions from the Chola period, a five-tiered rajagopuram (gateway tower), and is enclosed by a granite wall. The complex contains all the shrines, with the temple tank located outside the main entrance.

This shrine is also referred to as Saptamrita Kshetram (seven celebrated elements of nature), referring to seven of its elements such as Vimanam, Mandapam, Aaranyam, Tirtham, Kshetram, river, and town.

## Temple History:

During the churning of the ocean of milk (Thiruparkadal) by the Devas and Asuras, Goddess Lakshmi emerged with a garland for Lord Vishnu but felt too shy to present it in front of everyone. Seeking a private setting for their union, she began penance in Thirukanna Mangai. Moved by her devotion, Lord Vishnu appeared, and they prepared to marry. The Devas, eager to witness the event, arrived uninvited.

To ensure the wedding was private, Lord Vishnu transformed the Devas into honeybees. Goddess Lakshmi agreed to the marriage, pleased with their unobtrusive forms. Today, visitors can see two holes in the Thaayar Sannidhi (Goddess' sanctum), where honeycombs symbolise the Devas as honeybees during the divine wedding.

### Thirukanna Mangai Andan's Insight

Thirukanna Mangai Andan, a disciple of Nadhamuni, once saw two dogs fighting and their owners quarrelling. He reflected, "If people fight to protect their pets, why should we not trust Perumal (Lord Vishnu) to protect our souls? We should surrender our duties and protection to God."

# Special Highlights:

For ages, it has been believed that to attain mukti or eternal salvation, one need not be a scholar of all Vedas; instead, staying at this place for at least a single night would lead to mukti.

The age-old beehive is found in the Thaayar Sannidhi.

## Major Festivals:

During the Tamil month of Chittirai, Brahmotsavam, a 10-day festival, is celebrated, and the festival deity is taken in procession around the streets of the temple on different mounts each day.

# 17 THIRUKANNAPURAM

Thiru Kannapuram Temple (Sowriraja Perumal Temple)

- **Moolavar**: Sri Neelamega Perumal, Sowriraja Perumal Temple

- **Thaayar**: Kannapura nayagi Thaayar

- **Pushkarani**: Nitya pushkarani

- **Vimanam**: Utpalagatha Vimanam

- **Mangalasasanam**: Thirumangai Azhwar - 14 Paasurams.

- **Prathyaksham**: Kanva Maharishi, Thandaka Maharishi and Garudan.

- **Location**: This temple lies in the Tanjore district of Tamil Nadu. It is 4 miles from Nannilam Railway Station. From Mayavaram, one must go to Thirupugazhoor and from there, by crossing a river, Thirukannapuram is 1 mile away.

## Architectural Significance:

The temple is believed to have been constructed during the early Chola period, around the 9th century CE, making it over 1,100 years old. It has seen renovations and expansions by subsequent dynasties, including the Nayaks and the Vijayanagara rulers.

## Temple History:

### How Perumal got the name Sowri Perumal:

Once upon a time, the temple priest fell in love with a girl who came to the temple every evening to worship the Lord. One night before closing the temple garbhagraha, the priest gave the garland worn by Perumal to the girl. Unfortunately, the king arrived at the temple, and the priest was out of garlands to give him. The priest sent a boy to bring back the garland before the king completed his worship. The priest then gave the garland to the king as a token of respect. The king found a strand of hair in the garland and became angry with the priest. The poor priest told the king that it was Perumal's hair. The king said he would come and verify if Perumal had real hair. The next day, he came and pulled the hair, and a drop of blood spilled from Perumal. The king then realised the priest did not lie.

It is believed that Lord Sowri Perumal appeared as a 16-year-old boy and saved people from Ubari Charavasu, who started killing people.

### The Scar on Sowri Perumal's Forehead:

As per a legend, the original structure extended up to seven compounds and 13 miles leading to the seashore. The ruling Chola ruler was against Vaishnavism and wanted to destroy the temple. An ardent devotee pleaded with Vishnu to appear and destroy the ruler. Vishnu was unmoved, and in anger, the devotee threw a discus at the image, creating a scar. We can see the scar in the Vigraham even now.

## Major Festivals:

During "Maasi Magham" – a full moon day of the Tamil month of Maasi – Lord Sowri Perumal goes to Thirumalarayan Patinam for Theerthavari, which happens on the seashore.

On every new moon day, Perumal shows his walking style to Vibhishana (younger brother of Ravana).

# Special Offering:

Muniyadharayam Pongal

# 18 THIRUKANNANKUDI

- **Moolavar:** – Sri Damodara Narayana Perumal, Sri Samamameni Perumal, Sri Loga Narayana Perumal

- **Thaayar:** Sri Loga Nayaki Thaayar, Sri Aravindanayagi Thaayar

- **Pushkarani:** Shravana Pushkani

- **Vimanam:** Utpalathaga Vimanam

- **Mangalasasanam:** Thirumangai Azhwar-10 Paasurams.

- **Prathyaksham:** Bhrigu Maharishi, Brahma devan, Uparisaravasu, Gowtha Marishi, Thirumangai Azhwar.

- **Location:** This temple lies in the Tanjore district of Tamil Nadu. It's about 2 miles away from Keevalur Railway Station. On the Naagapatinam to Sikkal (or Keevalur) bus route, alight at Aazhiyur stop, and from there it's 3/4 miles away.

## Temple History:

### The Legend of Vashishtar and the Butter Idol

Vashishtar, a devoted sage, worshipped Lord Krishna by crafting a butter idol daily. One day, Krishna, amused by Vashishtar's devotion, took the form of a toddler and began eating the butter idol. Vashishtar, arriving for his prayers, found the idol gone and a small child running away with butter remnants. Curious, he chased the child. Other rishis, thinking they were helping, caught and tied the child's legs. When Vashishtar arrived,

Krishna revealed his true divine form as Lord Narayana.

## The Legend of Thirumangai Azhwar and the Four Names

Thirukannangudi, a place of divine significance, is associated with four unique names that each tell a story of devotion, miracles, and divine interactions involving Thirumangai Azhwar.

## Uranga Puli (The Tree That Doesn't Sleep)

Once, Thirumangai Azhwar obtained a golden shrine from Nagapattinam to construct the giant compound wall of the Srirangam temple. On his journey, he rested at Thirukannangudi and, to safeguard the golden shrine, buried it under a tamarind tree. He implored the tree to stay awake and guard the treasure while he slept. Miraculously, the tree complied and stayed vigilant throughout the night, earning the name "Uranga Puli," meaning "the tamarind tree that doesn't sleep."

## Thola Vazhaku (The Case That Doesn't Get Resolved)

The next morning, the villagers confronted Thirumangai Azhwar, questioning his presence and claiming ownership of the land. He declared that the land belonged to him, stating that proof could be found in Srirangam. The villagers and Thirumangai Azhwar travelled back and forth between Thirukannangudi and Srirangam, but the dispute remained unresolved for an extended period. This prolonged and unresolved conflict led to the name "Thola Vazhaku," meaning "the case that doesn't get resolved."

## Oora Kinaru
## (The Well That Dried Up)

During his stay, Thirumangai Azhwar grew thirsty and requested water from a local girl. The girl, sceptical of his claim to the land, refused to provide him with water. Angered by her refusal and doubting his rightful ownership, Thirumangai Azhwar cursed the well, causing it to dry up permanently. This incident led to the name "Oora Kinaru," meaning "the well without water."

## Kaayaa Makizh
## (The Tree That Doesn't Age)

Thirumangai Azhwar, hungry and in need of sustenance, found solace under a Makizham tree, which provided him with prasadam (divine food). The tree's divine act of offering food to the saintly Azhwar led to the name "Kaayaa Makizh," meaning "the tree that doesn't age."

# 19 THIRU NAAGAI

- **Moolavar:** Sri Neelamega Perumal, Sri Soundararaja Perumal

- **Thaayar:** Sri Soundaryavalli Thaayar, Sri Gajalakshmi

- **Pushkarani:** Sara Pushkarani.

- **Vimanam:** Soundarya Vimanam

- **Mangalasasanam:** Thirumangai Azhwar - 10 Paasurams.

- **Prathyaksham:** Lord Brama, Naagarajan and Thirumangai Azhwar.

- **Location:** It is located in Nagapattinam, a town in the South Indian state of Tamil Nadu.

## Architectural Significance:

The temple, built by Pallavas, Nagars, and Cholas (8th-10th centuries), later received contributions from the Thanjavur Nayaks and Marathas. The Nayak king built the seven-tiered tower as a lighthouse. Key contributors include Jagul Nayakar, who built the tower and halls, and Kundo Pandithar, who added several shrines in 1737. Early 20th-century renovations were funded by local citizens and notable individuals. Inscriptions document these contributions.

## Temple History:

- **Krita Yuga:** Adhisesha, the divine serpent, worshipped Soundararaja Perumal. Lord Vishnu, impressed by Adhisesha's devotion, accepted him as his serpent bed. This place was named Nagapattinam, with "Naga" meaning serpent.

- **Treta Yuga:** Bhoomi Devi (Earth Goddess) worshipped Soundararaja Perumal, bringing immense blessings to the Earth and reaffirming her divine connection with Lord Vishnu.

- **Dwapara Yuga:** Sage Markandeya Maharishi worshipped Soundararaja Perumal, earning the Lord's grace and further sanctifying the temple.

- **Kali Yuga:** King Sali Sugan Maharaja worshipped Soundararaja Perumal, leading to miraculous events and enhancing the temple's grandeur.

### The Divine Interaction with Dhruva Maharaja

Dhruva Maharaja performed intense penance to see Lord Vishnu. When the Lord appeared, Dhruva was overwhelmed and speechless. Understanding this, Perumal touched Dhruva with his conch (sankha), giving him the ability to sing divine hymns.

# Special highlights:

Soundararaja Perumal is depicted with a bunch of keys at his hip, symbolising kingship and authority. He also wears a single blue stud in one ear, signifying his divine charm and uniqueness.

## Major Festivals:

During the Tamil month of Chittirai, the Hindu calendar is read at the temple, and the festival deity is taken in procession around Mada Street. Similar processions occur during the Maga star of Chittirai and Magam. In Aani, a five-day NammAzhwar festival is held. Soundaravalli Thaayar's ten-day festival in Aani features flag hoisting and chariot processions. Perumal joins Thaayar for their celestial wedding during Uthiram. In Aadi, a ten-day festival marks the summer solstice with Perumal's procession. Other major festivals include Krishna Jayanthi, Navaratri, Vaikuntha Ekadashi, and Vijayadashami. The temple also celebrates Manavala Mamunigal's festival in Purattasi and other significant festivals throughout the year, accompanied by traditional music and chariot processions.

# 20 TANJAI MAAMANIKKOYIL

**Thanjamamani Kovil**

- **Moolavar:** Sri Neelamega Perumal

- **Thaayar:** Sri Sengamala Valli Thaayar

- **Pushkarani:** Kannika Pushkarani (Vinnaru)

- **Vimanam:** Soundarya Vimanam

- **Prathyaksham:** Parasara Muni

**Manikundra Perumal**

- **Moolavar:** Sri Manikundra Perumal and

- **Thaayar:** Ambuja Valli Thaayar

- **Pushkarani:** Sri Rama Theertham

- **Vimanam:** Manikooda Vimanam

- **Prathyaksham:** Markandeya Maharishi

**Thanjai Aazhi Perumal**

- **Moolavar:** Sri Narasimha Perumal and

- **Thaayar:** Sri Thanjai Nayagi Thaayar

- **Pushkarani:** Surya Pushkarani

- **Vimanam:** Veda Sundara Vimanam

- **Mangalasasanam:** ThirumangaiAzhwar - 3 Paasurams, NammAzhwar - 1 Paasuram BhoodathAzhwar - 1 Paasuram.

## Temple History:

### The Demons' Terror and the Sage's Penance

During the Krita Yuga, King Madhu ruled the land. His reign was troubled by three fearsome demons: Thanjagan, Dhandagan, and Gajamugam. These demons disrupted the penance of Sage Parasara, who then prayed fervently to Lord Vishnu for protection.

### Thanjagan's Defeat

Lord Vishnu, responding to Sage Parasara's prayers, appeared on Garuda, his divine mount, and vanquished Thanjagan. Before his death, Thanjagan requested that the place be named in his memory. Hence, the temple and the region came to be known as Tanjai.

### Gajamugam's Defeat

To defeat Gajamugam, Lord Vishnu took the form of Narasimha, the man-lion. In this fierce form, he destroyed the demon, and the shrine was named Thanjai Aazhi Perumal in remembrance of this victory.

### Dhandagan's Defeat

Finally, Lord Vishnu assumed the form of Varaha, the white boar, to vanquish Dhandagan. After defeating Dhandagan, Lord Vishnu emerged at Srimushnam, and the region was named Dhandaka Vanam in memory of the event.

## Special Highlights:

This Divyadesam is a collection of three temples, each within a distance of about one mile. All three Perumals are in a sitting posture, and all three Utsavars are named "Sriman Narayanan."

(This page intentionally left blank)

# 21 THIRUNANDIPURA VINNAGARAM

Thirunandipura Vinnagara Temple (Jagannatha Perumal Temple) also known as Champakaranya Kshetram

- **Moolavar:** Sri Jaganatha Perumal

- **Thaayar:** Sri Senbagavalli Thaayar.

- **Pushkarani:** Nandhi Theertham

- **Vimanam:** Mandhara Vimanam

- **Mangalasasanam:** ThirumangaiAzhwar - 10 Paasurams.

- **Prathyaksham:** Nandi and King Sibhi.

- **Location**: This place is in the Thanjore district of Tamil Nadu. And situated at a distance of 1 1/2 miles from Korukai.

## Architectural Significance:

Once the Chola capital, the temple benefited from their contributions. During the Thanjavur Nayaks' rule, Vijayaranga Chokkappa Nayak also contributed significantly. The Vanamamalai Mutt currently maintains and administers the temple.

## Etymology:

Nandhan means "Teacher" or "Guide." As Lord Narayana guided at this place, he is called "Nadhanadha."

## Temple History:

One of the significant legends associated with Nathan Kovil is the penance of Shenbaga Valli Thaayar, which took place at Champakaranya Kshetram. Thaayar desired to marry Perumal and to eternally reside in Lord Vishnu's chest. To fulfil this deep longing, she performed severe penance facing the East direction at this sacred site. Moved by her devotion and earnest desire, Lord Vishnu appeared before her and granted her wish. Thus, Shenbaga Valli Thaayar attained the honour of being perpetually present in the chest of Lord Vishnu.

## The Legend of Adhikara Nandhi

### Nandhi's Journey to Vaikunta

Adhikara Nandhi, the revered vehicle (vahana) of Lord Shiva, once wished to visit Lord Vishnu in Vaikunta. Filled with eagerness and devotion, Nandhi hurried to meet the Lord but was stopped by Vishnu's gatekeepers, Jaya and Vijaya. They denied him entry, and as a result, Nandhi was cursed with an unexplained heat in his body, causing him great discomfort.

### Seeking Lord Shiva's Guidance

Distressed, Nandhi returned to Lord Shiva and sought his advice. Understanding the gravity of the situation, Lord Shiva advised Nandhi to return to Lord Vishnu and seek his grace to relieve him of the curse.

## Nandhi's Penance and Redemption

Following Shiva's advice, Nandhi went back to Lord Vishnu and performed intense penance. Pleased with Nandhi's devotion and persistence, Lord Vishnu appeared before him and lifted the curse, restoring peace and comfort to Nandhi. The sacred tank at Nathan Kovil, Nandhi Thertha Pushkarani, is believed to have been created to alleviate Nandhi's heat and discomfort, symbolising purification and divine grace.

### Major Festivals:

Pavitrotsavam is a festival organised in the temple by Karimaran Kalai Kappagam of Triplicane, Chennai, every July. Akshaya Tritiya is another major festival celebrated in the temple when the festival deity is taken in procession on a Garuda mount around the temple.

# 22 THIRUVELLIYANKUDI

- **Moolavar:** Sri Kola Villi Raman and Sringara Sundarar

- **Thaayar:** Maragathavalli Thaayar

- **Pushkarani:** Sukra Theertham, Parasurama Theertham, Indra Theertham, Prasura Theertham

- **Vimanam:** Pushkalavartha Vimanam.

- **Mangalasasanam:** Thirumangai Azhwar - 10 Paasurams.

- **Prathyaksham:** Lord Shukran, Brahma, Indra, Parasara Maharishi, Mayan, Markandeya Maharishi and Bhoomi Piratti.

- **Location:** This temple lies in the District of Tanjore, Tamil Nadu. Reach Anaikarai from Kumbakonam and head towards Senganoor and the temple is about 3/4 miles away from this place. One can also be reached Via Chozhavaram, Muttakudi and Mayavaram.

## Architectural Significance:

The temple is believed to have been built by the Medieval Cholas, with later expansions by Vijayanagara kings.. There is a four-tiered rajagopuram, the temple's gateway tower, in the temple.

# Temple History

## Restoration of Sukracharya's Eye

Thiru Velliangudi is a sacred Kshetram where Lord Vishnu, in his Vamana avatar, restored the eye of Sukracharya, the preceptor of the Asuras. During the Vamana avatar, Sukracharya lost his eye while trying to obstruct the Lord's mission to subdue the demon king Mahabali. As an act of divine grace, Lord Vishnu restored Sukracharya's eye at this very place. The name "Thiru Velliangudi" is derived from Sukra (Velli) and the divine grace (Angudi) bestowed upon him.

## Mayan's Desire to Serve

Mayan, the architect of the Asuras, desired to serve Lord Vishnu by contributing to the architecture of his temples, a role usually reserved for Vishwakarma, the architect of the Devas. Lord Vishnu, recognising Mayan's devotion, appeared before him in his grand Vishvaroopam (universal form) with four hands and a majestic appearance.

## Vishwakarma's Request

Vishwakarma, witnessing this grand form, expressed his reluctance, saying he wished to see Lord Vishnu in a more familiar and approachable form. Responding to this, Lord Vishnu transformed into Kola Villi Raman, appearing as Lord Rama with two hands, showcasing his divine grace and accessibility to Mayan and all his devotees.

## Special Highlights:

Garudan, in this temple, has Sangu and Chakkaram in his hands, which will be generally found in the hands of the Perumal.

## Major Festivals:

Vishnupathi Punniya Kalam, an auspicious time during the first days of Tamil months of Vaikasi, Avani, Karthigai and Masi, is celebrated in the temple seeking divine auspices from Garuda.

# 23 THERAZHUNDUR

- **Moolavar:** Sri Devathi Rajan (Gosakan in Sanskrit, Aa Maruvi Appan in Tamil)

- **Thaayar:** Sri Sengamalavalli Thaayar

- **Pushkarani:** Darisana Pushkarani

- **Vimanam:** Garuda Vimanam

- **Mangalasasanam:** ThirumangaiAzhwar - 45 Paasurams

- **Prathyaksham:** Dharma devadai, Uparisaravasu, River Cauvery, Garudan and Agastiyar.

- **Location:** Situated in the Tanjore district of Tamil Nadu, it lies between Mayavaram Junction and Kuttalam, 7 km from Kuttalam and about 8 km from Mayavaram.

## Architectural Significance:

The original structure of the temple was built by the Karikala Chola during the 1st century CE, with later additions from the Cholas during the 11th century.

## Temple History:

### Thirumangai Azhwar's Devotion

Thirumangai Azhwar, one of the twelve revered Azhwars, composed 45 hymns dedicated to the deity of Therazhundur. He sent a message to Aa Maruvi Appan through a pigeon, expressing his longing for a divine marriage with Lord Vishnu.

## Birthplace of Poet Kambar

Therazhundur is also notable as the birthplace of the celebrated poet Kambar, who composed the Kambaramayanam. The temple honours Kambar with a shrine dedicated to him and his wife, as well as a Kambar Mandapam.

## Unique Depiction of Perumal

In this temple, Perumal is depicted alongside a cow and calf, which is a unique representation. Instead of the usual consorts Bhoo Devi and Sri Devi, Garuda and Prahladan are seen with the deity.

## The Story of King Uparacharavasu

King Uparacharavasu, known for his chariot that never touched the ground, once delivered a biased judgement. As a consequence, he lost his divine power, and his chariot's wheel was buried in the soil. This event led to the place being named Therazhundur, meaning "the place where the chariot sank" (Ther in Tamil means chariot, and Azhudu means sank).

## Vatsa Abaharna Charitram

According to the Bhagavatha Purana, Lord Brahma once stole calves from the village and took them to Brahma Lokha. In response, Lord Krishna transformed himself into all the calves for the villagers. While searching for the calves, he arrived at this place, liked it, and decided to stay, making Therazhundur a significant site.

## Garuda's Offerings

Garuda offered two crowns to Lord Vishnu. The first was the Vairamudi, now in Melkote (Thiru Narayana Puram), where a famous festival occurs annually during the Tamil month of Panguni. The second offering was the Vimana (a special ornament) for the temple at Therazhundur, where Garuda resides alongside Lord Vishnu.

## Prahlada's Wish

Prahlada, who witnessed the fierce form of Lord Narasimha during his avatara, wished to see him in a calm and composed appearance. This desire was fulfilled at Therazhundur, where the deity is depicted in a serene form.

## Thirumangai Azhwar's Encounter

Thirumangai Azhwar once attempted to cross Therazhundur without singing praises to Perumal. As he reached the pushkarani, his legs began to tremble, preventing him from moving further. Lord Devathi Rajan appeared as Aa Maruvi Appan with cows and calves, prompting the Azhwar to compose his hymns in reverence. The verse, "Thiruviku Thiruvagiya Selva Deivathukarase," celebrates this divine encounter.

## Kaveri Thaayar and Agasthiyar's Curse

The temple is also associated with the story of Kaveri Thaayar, where Perumal resolved the curse of Sage Agasthiyar, highlighting his role as a divine protector and healer.

# 24 THIRUCHIRUPULIYUR

- **Moolavar:** Sri Krupa Samuthra Perumal (also known as Aru Ma Kadal, Ocean of Mercy)

- **Thaayar:** Thirumamagal Nachiyar (Sri Dayanayagi Thaayar)

- **Pushkarani:** Manasa Pushkarani

- **Vimanam:** Nandha Vardhana Vimanam

- **Mangalasasanam:** Thirumangai Azhwar - 10 Paasurams.

- **Prathyaksham:** Vyasa Maharishi and ViyagraPada rishi.

- **Location:** This temple lies in the Tanjore district of Tamil Nadu. It's about 2 miles from Kollumankudi, which is on the Aranthangi - Mayavaram railway route.

## Temple History:

### The Legends of Chirupuliyur Appearance and Divine Mercy

In Chirupuliyur, Lord Perumal appears as a small and cute child in the reclining posture known as Bala Sayanam. Despite his small form, he is known for his boundless mercy, earning the name Aru Ma Kadal and Krupa Samuthra Perumal, symbolising the ocean of compassion. Thirumangai Azhwar, moved by the divine mercy of Perumal, composed 10 hymns in praise of this deity.

## Adhishesan's Separate Shrine

The temple features a separate sannidhi (sanctum) for Adhishesan, the divine serpent on whom Lord Vishnu rests. This unique feature underscores the temple's significance and the special reverence given to Adhishesan.

## Vyagrapada Rishi's Quest

Rishi Vyagrapada, known for his devotion, once sought Lord Nataraja's guidance on who could grant moksha (liberation). Lord Nataraja brought Vyagrapada to Chirupuliyur, indicating that Krupa Samuthra Perumal holds the power to bestow liberation. The name "Vyagrapada" means "tiger-footed," symbolising his swift and determined journey to the temple.

## The Conflict Between Adhishesan and Garuda

## The Fight and Resolution

Once, Adhishesan and Garuda engaged in a fierce argument over who was more powerful. To resolve the conflict, Adhishesan travelled across the world and eventually came to Chirupuliyur. Here, Lord Perumal granted Adhishesan a place of honour within the temple, symbolising peace and reconciliation.

## Special Highlights:

Similar to the deity at Srirangam, Krupa Samuthra Perumal faces the south direction in Chirupuliyur, a unique feature that signifies his watchful protection and divine grace towards his devotees.

## Major Festivals:

Three daily rituals and three yearly festivals are held at the temple, of which the Brahmotsavam festival celebrated.

# 25 TALAICHCHANGA NAANMADIYAM

- **Moolavar:** Sri Vensudar Perumal (also known as Nan Madiya Perumal)

- **Thaayar:** Sri Thalai Changa Nachiyar

- **Pushkarani:** Chandra Pushkarani

- **Vimanam:** Chandra Vimanam

- **Mangalasasanam:** Thirumangai Azhwar 1 Paasuram

- **Prathyaksham:** Chandran (Moon god), Deva Bhridangar, Deva's Nitya suri's.

- **Location:** It is about 2 miles away on the route towards Seerkazhi. and 7 Km away from Kaviripoompatinam.

## Etymology:

During the Sangam period, Tamil people frequently visited the sea near this temple to take their ritual baths. The area was also a hub for sea shell trade, contributing to the name "Talaichanga Naanmadiyam," which refers to the head (thalai) of the conch (sanga) and the lunar association (naan madiyam).

## Temple History:

### The Legends of Talaichchanga Naanmadiyam

### The Curse of Chandran

Chandran (the Moon god) faced a severe curse due to his partiality towards one of his wives. Daksha Prajapati, who was the father of Chandran's 27 wives (representing the 27 Nakshatras or stars), noticed that Chandran favoured Rohini above all his other daughters. Angered by this favouritism, Daksha Prajapati cursed Chandran with Chayarogam, a wasting disease that caused his brilliance to fade.

### Chandran's Redemption

In his quest to rid himself of the curse, Chandran arrived at Talaichchanga Naanmadiyam. Here, he bathed in the sacred Chandra Pushkarani and performed intense penance to Vensudar Perumal. Moved by Chandran's devotion, Vensudar Perumal (Nan Madiya Perumal) blessed him, restoring his health and brilliance. This divine act earned Vensudar Perumal the name "Chandra Sabha Hara Perumal," the one who removed Chandran's curse.

## Special Highlights:

There is a very precious Sangu (shell) for the Perumal and a beautiful idol of Sri Andal Naachiyar.

(This page intentionally left blank)

# 26 THIRU INDHALLUR

- **Moolavar:** Sri Parimala Ranganatha (also known as Sugantha Vana Nathan)

- **Utsavar:** Thiri Vikrama Narayanan.

- **Thaayar:** Sri Parimala Ranganayaki. Sugantha Vana Nachiyar (also known as Chandra Sabha Vimochana Valli)

- **Utsavar: Thaayar** Mattavizh Kuzhali.

- **Pushkarani:** Indhu Pushkarani

- **Vimanam:** Veda Amodha Vimanam

- **Mangalasasanam:** ThirumangaiAzhwar - 11 Paasurams.

- **Prathyaksham:** Chandiran (Moon god).

- **Location:** This temple lies in the Tanjore district of Tamil Nadu. (To reach it, cross the River Cauvery, which is to the North of Mayuram town, and the temple is in the northeast direction from Mayuram.) or (By crossing the River Cauvery, which is to the North of Mayuram town, the temple is in the northeast direction from Mayuram.)

## Etymology:

The name "Parimala" means "fragrant," highlighting the divine fragrance that emanates from the deity.

## Architectural Significance:

The central shrine, of the presiding deity Parimala Ranganathar, is made of 12 ft (3.7 m) green stone. The temple is believed to be of significant antiquity, with contributions at different times from the Medieval Cholas, Vijayanagara Empire, and Madurai Nayaks. The Dvajasthamba Mandapam and Garuda Mandapam have sculpted pillars, with the latter having images of ten avatars of Vishnu.

## Temple History:

Thiru Indhalur Temple Legend: The Story of Parimala Ranganatha Perumal

### The Divine Fragrance of the Vedas

In ancient times, the Vedas were stolen by the demons Madhu and Kaitabha and became tainted, losing their divine fragrance. To restore their sanctity, Lord Vishnu cleansed the Vedas, removing all impurities and reinstating their divine aroma. Thus, the temple came to be known as Sugantha Vana Kshetram, symbolising the fragrant forest. The deity here is called Parimala Ranganatha Perumal, indicating the Lord who bestows divine fragrance. The Vimanam, or temple tower, is named Veda Amodha Vimanam, representing the sweet-smelling Vedas.

### The Unique Sayanam of Perumal

Parimala Ranganatha Perumal is depicted in a giant reclining posture (Sayana Thirukolam), holding the conch (shankha) and discus (chakra). This unique form is referred to as Vera Sayanam, highlighting the distinct posture and the divine weapons in his hands, not commonly seen in other Divya Desams.

# Thirumangai Azhwar's Encounter

## Azhwar's Anger and Perumal's Response

Thirumangai Azhwar, a great devotee and poet-saint, visited Thiru Indhalur at around 11: 45 AM, only to find the temple doors locked. The priest asked him to return in the evening. Frustrated, Azhwar shouted at Perumal, expressing his anger and disappointment. Perumal appeared before him and asked why he was so upset, noting that Azhwar, a true devotee, had never behaved this way before.

Azhwar replied that he had sung countless hymns in praise of Perumal but felt unrewarded for his devotion, stating, "Numai Thozhuthom - Inmaiku Inbam Pethom, vazhthe pom neere." He lamented that despite knowing all the rights and wrongs of the world, Perumal had forgotten him as a devotee.

Perumal responded calmly, reminding Azhwar of the blessings he had received, including the honour of being made an Azhwar. He explained that he had been residing in Azhwar's heart, guiding him to compose the beautiful hymns. Azhwar acknowledged this but expressed his desire for Perumal's presence in all aspects of his life.

## Major Festivals:

The major festival celebrated in the temple is the Chitrai festival, which is celebrated during the Tamil month of Chittirai. Other festivals in the temple include the 10-day Aaandal Aadi festival celebrated during July–August, Thaayar Navaratri Utsavam during the Tamil month of Purattasi (September–October), and the 10-day Aipasi Thula Mahostavam during Aipasi (October–November).

## Introduction to ThiruNaangur Divya Desams

ThiruNaangur is renowned for its cluster of 11 sacred temples, each a Divya Desam dedicated to Lord Vishnu. These temples are deeply intertwined with mythological events involving Lord Shiva and Goddess Parvati (Sati).

## The Origin of ThiruNaangur Divya Desams

The legend begins with a pivotal event in Hindu mythology. Goddess Sati, daughter of Daksha Prajapati, wished to attend her father's grand yagna (sacrificial ceremony). Lord Shiva, her consort, cautioned her against attending, predicting that she would be insulted. Ignoring Shiva's warning, Sati attended the yagna and faced grave humiliation. Overwhelmed by grief and anger, she immolated herself in the sacrificial fire.

Upon hearing this, Lord Shiva was engulfed in fury and began his fierce dance of destruction, the Rudra Tandavam. His wrathful dance shook the heavens and the Earth, and from his matted locks, he created 11 Rudra forms. These Rudras spread around the area of Seerkazhi, causing immense fear and disturbance among the sages and Devas.

## Lord Vishnu's Intervention

To pacify the enraged Rudras, the Devas and sages sought the help of Lord Vishnu. In response, Vishnu appeared in eleven different forms at eleven distinct places around ThiruNaangur, calming each Rudra with his divine presence. These places eventually became the ThiruNaangur Divya Desams, celebrated for their unique connection to both Vishnu and Shiva.

## The Eleven Temples of ThiruNaangur

1. Thiru Kaavalampaadi
2. Thiru Arimeya Vinnagaram
3. Thiru Vann Purushothamam
4. Thiru Semponsei Kovil
5. Thiru Manimaadakovil
6. Thiru Vaikuntha Vinnagaram
7. Thiru Devanar Thogai
8. Thiru Thetri Ambalam
9. Thiru Manikoodam
10. Thiru Vellakkulam
11. Thiru Paarthanpalli

Each of these temples hold a unique deity and distinct history, contributing to the rich tapestry of ThiruNaangur's spiritual heritage.

## The Grand Festival: Garudotsavam

A highlight of the ThiruNaangur Divya Desams is the world-famous Garudotsavam, also known as the 11 Garuda Seva Utsavam. This festival is celebrated during the Thai month on the new moon day (Amavasya). During this event, all eleven Perumal idols are mounted on Garuda vahanas (the eagle mount of Vishnu) and taken in a grand procession. The festival draws an enormous crowd, with approximately 50,000 to 60,000 devotees gathering to witness and participate in the celebrations. The atmosphere is charged with devotion, and the sight of the eleven Garudas together is both awe-inspiring and spiritually uplifting.

# 27 THIRUKAAVALAMPAADI

- **Moolavar:** Sri Gopala Krishnan with Rukmini and Satyabhama

- **Utsavar:** Thiri Vikrama Narayanan.

- **Thaayar:** Madavaral Mangai (Sengamala Nachiyar)

- **Utsavar: Thaayar:** Sri Mattavizh Kuzhali.

- **Pushkarani:** Thadamalar Poigai

- **Vimanam:** Swayambu Vimanam

- **Mangalasasanam:** ThirumangaiAzhwar - 10 Paasurams.

- **Prathyaksham:** Vishwaksenar (Senai Thalaivar) and Rudran.

## Etymology:

Thiru Kaavalampaadi, also known as Thiru Kaavalam Paadi, is one of the significant Divya Desams dedicated to Lord Vishnu. The name 'Kaavalampaadi' is derived from the word 'Kaavu,' meaning garden, signifying the divine garden associated with this temple.

# Temple History

## The Legend of Narakasura and Indra's Garden

The temple's mythology is deeply rooted in the story of Narakasura, a demon who stole the earrings (Kundalam) of Aditi Devi and the celestial umbrella (Kodai). In response to the cries for help from Aditi Devi and the celestial beings, Lord Krishna, accompanied by his consort Satyabhama, embarked on a mission to vanquish Narakasura. After a fierce battle, Krishna defeated Narakasura and retrieved the stolen items, returning them to Indra, the king of the Devas.

Following this victory, Satyabhama expressed a desire to possess the Parijatha flower from Indra's garden. When Krishna approached Indra with the request, Indra refused to part with the flower. Angered by Indra's refusal, Krishna decided to create an even more magnificent garden for Satyabhama. This garden was established in Thiru Kaavalampaadi, earning the place its name, which signifies a beautiful garden.

The main deity, Gopala Krishnan, is depicted with his consorts, Rukmini and Satyabhama. This divine trio is a rare and unique representation, highlighting the temple's special significance in the worship of Krishna.

Madavaral Mangai, also known as Sengamala Nachiyar, is the Thayar (goddess) of this temple. Devotees believe that she grants boons and fulfills the wishes of those who pray with devotion.

(This page intentionally left blank)

# 28 THIRUKAZHICHEERAMA VINNAGARAM

- **Moolavar:** Sri Thirivikaraman Also known as Thadalan and Ulagalanthan.

- **Utsavar:** Thiri Vikrama Narayanan.

- **Thaayar:** Sri Loga Nayaki

- **Utsavar: Thaayar** Sri Mattavizh Kuzhali.

- **Pushkarani:** Sanga Pushkarani, Chakara Theertham.

- **Vimanam:** Pushkala Vartha Vimanam.

- **Mangalasasanam:** ThirumangaiAzhwar - 10 Paasurams.

- **Prathyaksham:** Ashta Kona Maharishi.

- **Location:** This temple lies in Seerkazhi in the Mayiladuthurai district of Tamil Nadu. It's about half a mile away from the Seerkazhi station.

## Etymology:

Kazhi: Refers to the removal or destruction of sins. Seer: Means to remove or destroy. Kazhicheer: Signifies a temple that destroys all sins.

## Architectural Significance:

The temple is believed to have been built by the Cholas, with later contributions from the Medieval Cholas, Vijayanagara kings, and Madurai Nayaks.

## Temple History:

### Romasa Muni's Penance:

Romasa Muni performed severe penance as Brahma had become arrogant. Perumal granted a boon to Romasa Muni stating that each time one of his hairs fell, Brahma would lose a year of his lifespan. This caused Brahma to realise his mistake and correct his arrogance. Visiting this temple is believed to destroy all sins and impart good thoughts to devotees.

### Vishwamithra and Lord Rama:

On the journey to Sidhasramam (present-day Buxar in Bihar) with Lord Rama and Lakshmana, Vishwamithra encountered the demoness Thadakai, who was destroyed by Rama.

### Thirumangai Azhwar and Thirugyana Sambandar's Competition:

During a poet competition between Thirumangai Azhwar and the famous Saiva poet Thirugyana Sambandar, Thirumangai Azhwar needed a Perumal to sing about. The villagers informed him that Perumal was hidden inside a sawdust pot by an old woman during tough times. Thirumangai Azhwar sang "Thadalava Thadalava…" to call Perumal, who emerged from the pot crawling and sat on Azhwar's thigh. With Perumal by his side, Thirumangai Azhwar won the competition.

## Special Highlights:

Thirumangai Azhwar won a challenge against Saiva Pulavar Sambandar by composing Paasurams in praise of the God in this temple.

## Major Festivals:

The major festival celebrated in the temple is the 10-day Vaikasi Brahmotsavam, held during the Tamil month of Vaikasi (May–June).

# 29 THIRU ARIMEYA VINNAGARAM

- **Moolavar:** Sri Kudamaadum Koothar
- **Utsavar:** Sri Gopalakrishnan
- **Thaayar:** Sri Amirtha Gadavalli Nachiyar
- **Pushkarani:** Kodi Theertham
- **Vimanam:** Uchasringa Vimanam
- **Mangalasasanam:** Thirumangai Azhwar - 10 Paasurams.
- **Prathyaksham:** Uthanga Maharishi.

## Temple History:

### The Devine conversation of Uthanga Maharishi.

After the Mahabharata events, Lord Krishna walked swiftly towards Dwaraka. Uthanga Maharishi stopped him and asked, "Where are you going, Kanna?"

Krishna replied, "It's all done. The Pandavas won the battle, and the Kauravas were defeated."

Maharishi questioned, "Why did the Pandavas win and the Kauravas lose?"

Krishna answered, "Because the Kauravas committed sins and the Pandavas performed good deeds."

Maharishi further probed, "Why did the Pandavas do good things and the Kauravas do bad things?"

Krishna explained, "It was because of their prior karma, the sins and virtues of their previous births. I don't have time to discuss this further; I need to go to Dwaraka."

Maharishi persisted, "It's not just because of their karma. It's because of your divine will. I heard you showed your Vishwaroopam to Arjuna. Can you show it to me as well?"

Krishna then revealed his Vishwaroopam and began dancing with an Amrutha Kudam (pot of nectar) on his head.

## The Story of Vinathai and Kathru

Vinathai, the mother of Garuda, and Kathru, the mother of the Nagas, had a dispute. There was a white horse, and Vinathai asked Kathru about its colour. Kathru claimed it was black. Puzzled, Vinathai questioned how Kathru could say that. Kathru proposed a challenge: if she could prove the horse was black, Vinathai would become her servant. Vinathai accepted.

Kathru ordered all the black cobras to tangle in the horse's tail, making it appear black. Feeling she had lost the challenge, Vinathai was dismayed. Kathru then stipulated that if Vinathai wanted to avoid being her servant, Garuda had to bring the Amrutha Kudam (pot of nectar).

Garuda managed to obtain the Amrutha Kudam, but before giving it to Kathru, Perumal took it and started dancing with the pot on his head. Krishna is known for his mastery in Koravai Koothu and Kudakoothu dance forms. Kudakoothu involves juggling the pot with his hands without disturbing the one on his head, all while playing the beri instrument tied to his hip.

## Special Highlights:

The idol of Moolavar is of the type Sudai Vadivam and is made from burnt clay; hence, only Thailakaapu is allowed here, and no thirumanjanam is done.

# 30 THIRUVANPURUSHOTTAMAM

Thiruvanpurushottamam Temple
(Purushottama Perumal Temple)

- **Moolavar:** Sri Purushothaman

- **Thaayar:** Sri Purushothama Nayaki

- **Pushkarani:** Sri Thiruparkadal Theertham

- **Vimanam:** Sri Sanjeeva Vigraha Vimanam

- **Mangalasasanam:** Thirumangai
  Azhwar - 10 Paasurams.

- **Prathyaksham:** Upamanyu Maharishi.

## Temple History:

### The Story of Vyagarapadhar and Upamanya

Vyagarapadhar, a devotee known for his dedication to performing flower services (pusha kaikaryam) for Lord Purushottaman, used to collect flowers for worship. One day, he left his son Upamanya at the temple and went to gather flowers. Upamanya, feeling scared and alone in his father's absence, started crying. Hearing his cries, Purushothama Nayaki Thaayar was moved by compassion and urged Lord Purushottaman to bring milk from the celestial ocean, Thiruparkadal, to calm the child. Perumal obliged, and Upamanya stopped crying, comforted by the divine milk.

### Thirumangai Azhwar's Hymns

Thirumangai Azhwar, one of the revered Azhwars, has sung beautiful hymns praising this temple and the deity, emphasising the compassionate nature of the divine couple and their care for devotees.

# 31 THIRUSEMPONSEI KOYIL

- **Moolavar:** Sri Hema Rangar / Sri Ponarangan

- **Thaayar:** Sri Allimalar Nachiyar

- **Pushkarani:** Sri Nithya Pushkarani

- **Vimanam:** Sri Kanaka Valli Vimanam

- **Mangalasasanam:** Sri ThirumangaiAzhwar - 10 Paasurams.

- **Prathyaksham:** Ekadasa Rudhirar

- **Etymology:** Sempon meaning gold, Semponsei Kovil- means Temple made of gold

## Temple History:

### The Story of Lord Rama and the Golden Cow

The name Semponsei Koyil translates to "Temple made of gold," with "Sempon" meaning gold. This temple is dedicated to Hema Rangar (Ponarangan), which refers to the beautiful form of the deity worshipped by Lord Rama.

After Lord Rama destroyed Ravana, who was a Brahmin by birth, he incurred Brahmahathi Dosham (the sin of killing a Brahmin). Seeking a way to rid himself of this sin, he approached Dhridanethrar Muni, who was performing penance at this temple. The sage advised Rama to construct a large golden cow and to stay inside it for four days. This ritual is called Goprasavam, symbolising rebirth from a cow. After emerging from the cow, Rama was instructed to perform generous acts of charity and finally donate the cow itself.

Following these instructions, Lord Rama performed the Goprasavam, emerged cleansed of his sin, and gave away the golden cow as part of his charity. Dhridanethrar Muni, who received the cow from Rama, used it to build the temple, thus giving it the name Semponsei Koyil.

## Special Highlights:

Among the 108 Kshetrams, This is the Only Divyadesam Where the Perumal Himself Gave the Money to Construct His Own Temple.

(This page intentionally left blank)

# 32 THIRU MANIMAADA KOVIL

- **Moolavar: Sri Narayana Perumal, Alatharku Ariyan**

- **Thaayar: Sri Pundariga Valli Thaayar**

- **Pushkarani:** Ruthra Pushkarani

- **Vimanam:** Pranava Vimanam

- **Mangalasasanam:** Thirumangai Azhwar - 12 Paasurams

- **Prathyaksham:** Lord Indra and Ekadasa Rudhirar

## Temple History:

### Lord Narayana's Teachings and Divine Appearance

The deity of Thiru Manimaada Koyil is Narayana Perumal, who is the same Lord Narayana that preached the sacred Thirumandhiram at Badarikasramam. This temple holds the distinction of being the first ThiruNaangur Divya Desam where Lord Narayana appeared to calm down the enraged Lord Shiva.

## Connection with Thirukotiyur Nambi and Shri Ramanujar

Thirukotiyur Nambi, a revered acharya of Shri Ramanujar, visited this temple to learn the Mandira Upadesam (sacred teachings). He later imparted this knowledge to Shri Ramanujar. Thirukotiyur Nambi has a dedicated sannidhi (shrine) within this temple, highlighting its historical and spiritual significance.

## Unique Features of Narayana Perumal

Narayana Perumal is depicted with the Prayoga Chakram, signifying his readiness to protect his devotees. The temple is also the focal point for the famous 11 Garuda Seva during the Tamil month of Thai. On this auspicious day, the deities from the other ten ThiruNaangur Divya Desams arrive at this temple on Garuda Vahanam, and Thirumangai Azhwar performs Mangalasasanam (divine praise). Additionally, Manavala Mamunigal performs Mangalasasanam for Thirumangai Azhwar.

## Legends of Rudra and Indra

**Lord Rudra's Penance:** To rid himself of the Brahmahathi Dosam (sin of killing a Brahmin), Lord Rudra (Shiva) came to this temple and performed penance.

**Indra's Penance:** Lord Indra, seeking to overcome a curse, also performed penance at this temple. Additionally, Indra's vehicle, Airavata (referred to as Naga in Sanskrit), did penance here to be freed from a curse. This association with Naga is why the area is named Naangur.

## Special Highlights:

On every day after Thai Amavasai, all the Perumals of the eleven ThiruNaangur Thirupathis come here to Manimaada Kovil in their Garuda Vahanams. On that occasion, Thirumangai Azhwar with his wife Kumudhavalli would come from Thirunagari along with the deity he worshipped. Then, the 11 ThiruNaangur Divyadesa Perumals are praised with the Paasurams (i.e., the Mangalasasanam made by him is sung) and finally, the Thiru Andikaapu is performed.

Thirumangai Azhwar would then accept the garlands and honour from each Perumal. Finally, all would set out on a grand procession.

# 33 THIRU VAIKUNTHA VINNAGARAM

- **Moolavar:** Sri Vaikunda Nathan (Thamarai Kannudaya Piraan)

- **Thaayar:** Sri Vaikunda Valli Thaayar (inside the Garbhagriha, like in Vaikuntham)

- **Pushkarani:** Lakshmi Pushkarani, Viraja Theertham

- **Vimanam:** Anantha Sathya Vardaga Vimanam

- **Mangalasasanam:** Thirumangai Azhwar - 10 Paasurams.

- **Prathyaksham:** King Uparisaravasu and Udhanga Maharishi.

## Temple History:

### Perumal Appearing as in Vaikuntham

Lord Vaikunda Perumal appears in a form resembling his appearance in Vaikuntham (the divine abode). This unique aspect gives the temple a special place among the Divya Desams.

### Thaayar: Inside the Garbhagriha

Unlike most temples where the goddess has a separate shrine, Vaikunda Valli Thaayar resides inside the Garbha Griha (sanctum sanctorum) with Vaikunda Perumal, akin to the divine couple in Vaikuntham.

## The Story of King Swetha Kethu

King Swetha Kethu reached Karya Vaikuntham (a preparatory stage before reaching actual Vaikuntham). However, he experienced human needs such as thirst and hunger, which puzzled him. Upon consulting Narada, he learned that his lack of charitable deeds and righteous acts on Earth were the reasons he could not fully transcend human needs even in Karya Vaikuntham.

## Remedy Suggested by Narada

Narada advised the king to visit Vaikuntha Vinnagaram and perform penance. Following Narada's advice, King Swetha Kethu performed intense penance at this temple. Lord Vaikunda Perumal, pleased with the king's devotion, appeared to him as he would in Vaikuntham, thereby granting him the vision of the divine abode.

# Special Highlights:

The temple has the pious river Viraja, which is considered to run across the border of Vaikunda Loga as the theertham.

(This page intentionally left blank)

# 34 THIRUVAALI AND THIRUNAGARI

## Thiruvaali

- **Moolavar:** Sri Lakshmi Narasimha Perumal

- **Thaayar:** Sri Amirthavalli Thaayar (or Purna Valli Thaayar)

- **Pushkarani:** Sri Laakshana Pushkarani

- **Vimanam:** Sri Ashtakshara Vimanam (also called Kesar Akiya Vimanam)

- **Mangalasasanam:** 42 Paasurams by Kulasekara Azhwar and Thirumangai Azhwar

- **Prathyaksham:** Thirumangai Azhwar

## Etymology:

"Thiru" means Lakshmi, and "Aali" is a short form of Aalinganam, meaning hugging, hence the name Thiruvaali.

## Temple History:

### Legend and Significance:

Narasimha's Calmness: After defeating Hiranyakashipu, Narasimha Perumal didn't calm down. Brahma and the Devas worshipped Perumal, who then settled in Thiruvaali with Lakshmi Devi on his right thigh. Typically, Lakshmi sits on Perumal's left lap, but here, she is on his right.

## Marriage of Amirtha Valli and Perumal:

Poorna Maharishi performed penance for a long time and had a daughter named Amirtha Valli, who married Vailali Mainthan (Perumal in Thirunagari). The marriage occurred in the Panguni month, and they were taken in a Moodu Pallaku (a decorated palanquin).

## Thiru Vedu Pari Utsavam:

This festival occurs the day before Panguni Uthiram, coinciding with the Brahmotsavam in Srirangam.

## Thirumangai Azhwar's Transformation:

Before becoming an Azhwar, Thirumangai Azhwar was known as Neelan. He needed to provide annadhanam (food donation) for 1000 people daily, as promised to Kumudha Valli, but lacked the means. Thus, he resorted to robbery.

Neelan had four skilled assistants:

- Neermel Nadapan: Could walk on water.
- Nizhalil Othuguvan: Could walk in others' shadows and steal.
- Thazhooduvan: Could open locks by blowing air.
- Thozhavazhakan: Would win all legal cases.

They identified a rich couple adorned with jewels travelling in a palanquin Moodu Pallaku as a prime target. Late at night, Thirumangai Azhwar approached them, demanding their jewels. The bride and groom were actually Perumal and Thaayar in disguise. When Azhwar tried to lift the stolen goods, the bag became incredibly heavy.

## Revelation and Transformation:

Perumal, in disguise, taught Thirumangai Azhwar the Thirumanthram (sacred mantra). Realising the identity of the couple, Thirumangai Azhwar repented and understood his divine purpose. This encounter transformed him into Thirumangai Azhwar.

# Thirunagari

- **Moolavar:** Sri Vedaraja Perumal (Kalyana Rangaraja Perumal), also known as Vayalali Mainthan

- **Thaayar:** Sri Amirthavalli Nachiyar

- **Pushkarani:** Haladhini Pushkarani

- **Vimanam:** Ashtakshara Vimanam

# Temple History;

## Lakshmi Devi's Separation and Reunion:

In Krithayuga, Lakshmi Devi separated from Perumal and hid in a lotus in Haladhini Pushkarani at Thirunagari. With thousands of lotuses in the pond, it was difficult to find her. Perumal, whose right eye is the sun and left eye is the moon, opened his left eye. This caused all the flowers to blossom except the one hiding Lakshmi Devi. Thus, Perumal identified and reunited with Thaayar.

## King Ubaricharavasu's Penance:

In Trethayuga, King Ubaricharavasu's chariot stopped flying over Thirunagari. He performed penance, seeking moksha. Perumal appeared and informed him that he must wait until Kaliyuga to attain liberation.

## King Sangapala's Moksha:

In Dwaparayuga, King Sangapala visited Thirunagari during his conquest and sought sayujya moksha from Perumal, who granted him liberation.

## Special Highlights:

### Thirumangai Azhwar and Ramanuja's Connection:

The shrine of Bhagavat Ramanuja is located under Thirumangai Azhwar's shrine in Thirunagari, signifying the deep connection and reverence Ramanuja had for Thirumangai Azhwar.

There is a secret place known as Neenila Mutham in Thirunagari, where one can see the Vimanam of Thirukannapuram from there.

# 35 THIRU DEVANAAR TOGAI

- **Moolavar:** Sri Devanayaga Perumal

- **Utsavar:** Sri Madhava Perumal

- **Thaayar:** Sri Kadal Magal Nachiyar, Deivanayagi Thaayar, Sri Madhava Nayagi Thaayar

- **Pushkarani:** Shobana Pushkarani or Deva Sabha Pushkarani

- **Vimanam:** Shobana Vimanam

- **Mangalasasanam:** Thirumangai Azhwar - 10 Paasurams.

- **Prathyaksham:** Vashista Maharishi

- **Etymology:** The name Thiru Devanaar Togai comes from the gathering of all Devas (divine beings) who formed a group to worship Devanayaga Perumal at this sacred place. The unity and devotion of the Devas highlight the temple's significance as a site of divine assembly and veneration.

## Temple History:

### Emergence of Sri Devi Nachiyar

A profound event associated with this temple is the churning of the Ocean of Milk (Parkadal), where Sri Devi Nachiyar (Lakshmi) emerged. This divine occurrence led to her marriage with Perumal, symbolising the union of divine grace and supreme power.

## Special Highlights:

The Temple Gate Faces West and the Shadow of the Vimanam Falls Within the Vimanam Itself.

# 36 THIRUTTETRIAMBALAM

- **Moolavar:** Sri Senganmaal Ranganathar (Sri Lakshmi Renga Perumal)

- **Thaayar:** Sri Sengamala Valli Thaayar

- **Pushkarani:** Surya Pushkarani

- **Vimanam:** Veda Vimanam or Shrutivaya Vimanam

- **Mangalasasanam:** Thirumangai Azhwar - 10 Paasurams.

- **Prathyaksham:** Naachiyar and Aadhisheshan

## Etymology:

Thiruttetriambalam: The name combines "Thetri," meaning a raised landscape, and "Ambalam," meaning place.

## Temple History:

### Churning of the Ocean of Milk:

This temple shares its history with Thirumanikoodam. After churning the Ocean of Milk (Thiruparkadal), Perumal obtained Amudham (nectar). Deciding not to give it to the Asuras (demons), he took the form of Mohini and kept the Amudha Kudam (pot of nectar) on his hip.

### Trickery of the Asuras:

When serving the nectar, Perumal told the Asuras that he would serve the Devas first as they were smaller and childish, and the brave Asuras would get it last. The Asuras agreed, but soon realised the nectar might finish before their turn. Rahu and Ketu, sons of the Asura woman Simhika, took the form of Devas and sat in their queue. The Sun and Moon gods noticed this and informed Perumal. Perumal, using his chakra, chopped Rahu's head. Consequently, Rahu became headless and, to this day, seeks revenge by causing eclipses, catching hold of the Sun and Moon.

## Creation of Surya Pushkarani:

Out of fear of Rahu, the Sun god created the Surya Pushkarani. The Sun god hid in Surya Pushkarani, where Perumal blessed him in this temple.

## Hiranyachagan's Demise

Perumal planned to destroy the demon Hiranyachagan and went to a village called Kalakeyapuram. Sri Devi and Bhoomi Devi expressed their concern about their survival in his absence. Perumal assured them to stay near him in his Sayana Kolam (reclining posture) and keep thinking of him until his return.

# Special Highlights:

This is the Only Divya Desam in Thirunaangur Where Perumal is in a Sleeping Posture with Four Hands.

(This page intentionally left blank)

# 37 THIRUMANIKKOODAM

- **Moolavar:** Sri Varadaraja Perumal (Gajendra Varadha Perumal)

- **Utsavar:** Sri Manikooda Nayakan

- **Thaayar:** Sri Maamagal Naachiyar and Sri Bhoomi Piratti.

- **Pushkarani:** Chandra Pushkarani

- **Vimanam:** Kanaka VimanamTemple History

- **Mangalasasanam:** Thirumangai Azhwar - 10 Paasurams.

- **Prathyaksham:** Lord Chandran

## Temple History:

### Churning of the Ocean of Milk:

Similar to Thiruttetriambalam, this temple shares the history of the churning of the Ocean of Milk. Perumal obtained the Amudham (nectar) and decided not to give it to the Asuras. Taking the form of Mohini, he kept the Amudha Kudam (pot of nectar) on his hip.

### Trickery of the Asuras:

When serving the nectar, Perumal told the Asuras that he would serve the Devas first as they were smaller and childish, and the brave Asuras would get it last. The Asuras agreed but soon realised the nectar might finish before their turn. Rahu and Ketu, sons of the Asura woman Simhika, took the form of Devas and sat in their queue. The Sun and Moon gods noticed this and informed Perumal. Perumal, using his chakra, chopped off Rahu's head. Consequently, Rahu became headless and, to this day, seeks revenge by causing eclipses, catching hold of the Sun and Moon.

## Creation of Chandra Pushkarani:

Out of fear of Rahu, the Moon god created the Chandra Pushkarani. The Moon god hid in Chandra Pushkarani and received Perumal's blessings in this temple.

(This page intentionally left blank)

# 38 THIRUVELLAKKULAM

- **Moolavar:** Sri Annan Perumal (Srinivasa Perumal, brother of Thirupathi Venkatachala Perumal)

- **Utsavar:** Sri Srinivasa Perumal

- **Thaayar:** Sri Alarmel Mangai Nachiyar

- **Utsavar: Thaayar:** Sri Padmavathi Thaayar (Poovar Thirumagal)

- **Pushkarani:** Swetha Pushkarani

- **Vimanam:** Thathvadyothaga Vimanam

- **Mangalasasanam:** Ekadesa Rudhirar and Swetha Rajan.

- **Prathyaksham:** Ekadesa Rudhirar and Swetha Rajan.

## Temple History:

### Thirumangai Azhwar and Kumudha Valli Nachiyar:

Thirumangai Azhwar first saw Kumudha Valli Nachiyar at this temple. Kumudha Valli was a girl from Swargalokha who, along with her friends, visited the temple to pluck flowers for the deity. However, she was left alone when her friends returned to Swargalokha and had to stay in the temple overnight.

A doctor adopted and cared for her. Thirumangai Azhwar, enchanted by her, decided to marry her and approached her father. Her father, acknowledging Azhwar's status as a warrior, deferred the decision to Kumudha Valli.

Kumudha Valli agreed to marry Thirumangai Azhwar but set two conditions:

1. Thirumangai Azhwar had to undergo Pancha Samskaram.
2. He had to provide anna dhanam (food donation) for 1000 people every day for one year.

These events are commemorated at this temple. Even today, after the 11 Garuda Utsavam, Thirumangai Azhwar is taken to Thiruvellakkulam before returning to Thirunagari.

**Legend of Swethan and Dundhumaran:**

Swethan, son of Dundhumaran from a royal family, was cursed to die at the age of 9. Fearing this fate, Vashista Muni advised them to go to Thiruvellakkulam, bathe in the Swetha Pushkarani, and perform penance for one month.

Swethan performed penance from the Aipasi month, Sukla Paksha Dasami, to the Karthikai month, Sukla Paksha Ekadesi. Perumal appeared and blessed him with a long and healthy life.

Due to this legend, the temple is considered auspicious for performing marriage ceremonies, 60th-anniversary celebrations, and 80th-anniversary celebrations.

## Special Highlights:

This Divyadesam is known as "South Thirupathi". All the offerings due to the Thiru Venkadamudayan of Thirupathi can be offered here too.

This sthalam is the avathara sthalam of Kumudhavalli Naachiyaar (wife of Thirumangai Azhwar).

# 39 THIRUPPAARTANPALLI

- **Moolavar:** Sri Taamaraiyaal Kelvan Perumal
- **Utsavar:** Parthasarathy Perumal
- **Thaayar:** Thamarai Nayagi Thaayar, Shegamalavalli
- **Vimanam:** Narayana Vimanam
- **Pushkarani:** Kadga Pushkarani
- **Mangalasasanam:** Thirumangai Azhwar - 10 Paasurams.
- **Prathyaksham:** Parthan, Varunan and Ekadasa Rudhirar.

## Temple History:

This temple is associated with the Mahabharata hero Arjuna, who has a shrine dedicated to him here. Arjuna's encounter with the Sage Agasthiyar Munivar and his subsequent penance to Lord Krishna is a significant event linked to the temple's history. When Arjuna asked for water, the sage advised him to pray to Krishna. Arjuna's penance resulted in Krishna appearing and creating the Kadga Pushkarani with his sword.

## Special Highlights:

The presence of Lord Krishna and Arjuna together in a single shrine is a unique feature of this temple.

The temple also houses a rare depiction of both Lord Krishna and Lord Rama seated together on one Singasanam (throne).

# 40 THIRUCHITRAKOOTAM

- **Moolavar:** Sri Govindarajan Perumal

- **Utsavar:** Devadhidevan. Also known as Parthasarathy. He is in the sitting posture. Chitira Koodhathullan, Sri Rama in his Vanavasa Kolam

- **Thaayar:** Sri Pundaregavalli

- **Pushkarani:** Pundarega Pushkarani.

- **Vimanam:** Saathvega Vimanam.

- **Mangalasasanam:** Thirumangai Azhwar - 32 Paasurams, Kulasekara Azhwar - 11 Paasurams. Total - 43 Paasurams.

- **Prathyaksham:** Thillai Moovayiravar, Paanini, Padhanjali and Vyakpathra Maharishi.

## Architectural Significance:

Chidambaram Temple has undergone several renovations by the Pallava, Chola, Pandya, Vijayanagara, and Chera dynasties. The current structure mainly dates back to the 12th and 13th centuries, with later additions in a similar style.

During the period of Kulothunga Chola II, the Govindaraja idol was removed from the temple complex but was later found and reinstated by King Krishnappa Nayak (1564–1572).

The temple features nine gateways, with four towering pagodas (gopurams) on the East, South, West, and North sides, each with seven levels. The eastern pagoda is notable for its sculptures of all 108 postures (karnams) of Bharatanatyam, the Indian dance form.

## Temple History:

### The Divine Dance Competition

Lord Shiva and Goddess Parvati once held a dance competition to determine the better dancer. This event took place on a beautifully constructed stage called "Chitra Koodam," adorned with intricate statues created by the divine architect Vishwakarma.

Initially, the verdict favoured Lord Shiva, upsetting Goddess Parvati. She sought an unbiased judgement from Lord Vishnu, who agreed to oversee the competition impartially. Despite her best efforts, Parvati couldn't match the complexity of Shiva's dance, especially his iconic Urthvathandavam pose, where he picked up his earring with his foot and placed it back on his ear.

The audience and Lord Vishnu declared Shiva the winner. Frustrated and unable to accept her defeat, Parvati transformed into Goddess Kali and took residence in the Thillai Moovayiravar temple.

## The Demons and the Divine Intervention

Long ago, three demons named Thanjagan, Dhandagan, and Gajamugam, along with their sisters Dhilli and Gilli, challenged Lord Vishnu. The formidable demons wreaked havoc, and their sisters supported them in their misdeeds. To restore peace and righteousness, Lord Vishnu decided to intervene.

He sent Gilli to Srimushnam to perform kainkaryam (divine service). As for Dhilli, Lord Vishnu transformed her into a Gandhara Maram (a special tree), which later became known as the Thillai tree.

## Special Highlights:

Thiruchitrakoodam is inside the premises of the Thillai Nataraja Temple, popularly known as Chidambaram Temple.

# GLOSSARY OF TERMS

Aradhanam: Ritual worship or service to the deity.

Brahmahathi Dosham: A sin incurred by killing a Brahmin.

Brahmotsavam: A grand festival celebrated in many South Indian temples.

Dakshanayana: The six-month period when the sun travels southward in its apparent path.

Dwadasi: The twelfth day of the lunar fortnight, significant for religious observances.

Ekadasi: The eleventh day of the lunar fortnight, observed with fasting by devotees of Lord

Homa: A fire ritual involving offerings to the sacred fire.

Mangalasasanam: Hymns sung in praise of the deity by the Azhwars.

Prasadam: Sanctified food offered to the deity and distributed to devotees.

Prathyaksham: Divine vision

Pushkarani: Sacred water or a holy water body associated with a temple.

Sannidhi: The sanctum or shrine within a temple.

Thayar: The consort of the main deity, typically referring to Lakshmi or other goddesses.

Utsavar: The festival deity taken out in processions during temple festivals.

Utharayana: The six-month period when the sun travels northward in its apparent path.

Vimanam: The tower above the sanctum of a temple.

Yajna: A Vedic ritual of offerings accompanied by chanting of Vedic mantras.

# THE JOURNEY CONTINUES

This is just the beginning of a larger journey exploring the divine realms of the 108 Divya Desams. In this volume, we've uncovered the stories, art, and architectural marvels of the first 40 temples. The next volume will take you further into the spiritual and artistic wonders of the remaining Divya Desams.

I warmly invite you to join me as we continue this exploration, delving deeper into the heritage and beauty of these sacred sites. Stay connected, and feel free to share your thoughts, feedback, or experiences—I'd love to hear from you!

**Contact Information:**
**Website**: www.heritageart.in
**Instagram**: @shanmugam.palani
**Email**: sayhello.to.shan@gmail.com

Thank you for accompanying me on this journey. Let's continue to celebrate and preserve the timeless legacy of the Divya Desams together!